CONTENTS

CREATIVE PROJECTS FOR THE HOME

Are you looking for something to do around the house this weekend? Here is just the book. *Creative Projects for the Home* from the *Better Homes and Gardens* library is chock full of things to make which will add comfort, value and aesthetic appeal to the home as well as giving the project builder an enormous sense of satisfaction.

Better Homes and Gardens

CREATIVE PROJECTS FOR THE HOME

Weekend projects with easy-to-follow plans, instructions and step-by-step pictures for the creative homemaker.

IN THE GARDEN

OUTDOOR STRUCTURES FOR SHELTER AND SUN

Build somewhere to play, to pot, to loll, to shelter from the searing heat of summer or catch the sun during the cooler months. Magnanimous hosts can turn their carpentry talents to projects to improve the garden for outdoor entertaining. Let a well developed sense of hospitality initiate good works in the garden by all means, but happily (and naturally enough) the residents will be the prime beneficiaries of any new garden structures. The house value will increase too.

Whatever springs up in the garden, be it pergola, pathway or barbecue, it will become part of the overall landscape. Give careful thought to its position in relation to the house and entry points to the garden as well as shade and sun in all seasons. Eating areas outdoors should be within a reasonable distance of the kitchen — some vital implement or seasoning is always forgotten. And as far as walking is concerned, a wiggly path may look quaint but the logical course between two points is a straight line. If a path is to follow an indirect course, plant trees and shrubs beside it to justify the chosen route.

Outdoor structures have to cope with the stresses of exposure to sun and rain so choose timbers with a reputation for weather resistance and apply suitable preservative finishes. Timber and the earth aren't always a wise mix. Again, select rot-resistant materials or elevate timber posts with brackets set into concrete.

In these outdoor projects, the methods of construction, finishes and, in the case of bricks, the stretcher bonding (the pattern resulting from the most common form of brick laying) form a practical and rather unadorned style. Details are fairly bland and don't strongly imply any particular architectural period but could be further simplified or, conversely, made more intricate to suit the style of the house. The garden and its accompanying structures should work as an extension of the house, both visually and practically. Pay particular attention to the heights of pergolas; use the height of the guttering on a bungalow or a line designating the junction of ground and first floors as a guide.

A pergola making a graceful and practical link between house and garden (see page 13)

ARBOUR

This set design for television creates the illusion of the great outdoors inside a film studio — change the illusion into reality in your own backyard.

The structure is built on a paved surface. If yours is to be located outside you should set each of the posts in galvanised post brackets in concrete footing pads. In that case, to avoid dry rot, replace the front of the seat (the bottom frame and seat verticals) with diagonal seat supports attached to the lower section of the top frame front and each of the posts.

Stand the posts, propping them temporarily to check for vertical. Nail the front, back and end barge boards in place. Lay two of the rafters on the ground to establish the angles of the cuts necessary to allow them to fit onto both the ridge and the barge boards. Cut out all 14 rafters (see diagram). Stand the rafters and ridge in place and nail at each junction.

Begin the seat by nailing the bottom frame pieces in place, using half-lap joints. Skew-nail the seven seat verticals in place. Nail in position to the front posts. Start the top frame by nailing first the long back frame in place, then the short back components. Follow these with the front short lengths and then the 2100 mm-long front piece. Insert the end and back struts last. Nail the chocks to the sides of the posts — one inside the two outer back posts and one each side of the central back post (see diagram).

Lay the seat slats using a 10 mm spacer and 60 mm-long nails on both horizontal and vertical surfaces. Round off one corner of the 50 x 25 mm timber and use as trim around the front edge of the seat.

To finish the structure, use prefabricated lattice, purchased after you have completed the rest of the structure. Frame each section with 75 x 38 mm timber, by tacking the lattice to the rear of the frame. Position the panels 300 mm from the top of the posts, and nail the frames onto the posts. Paint the structure in colours of your choice.

The lattice frame and rafters in position.

You could extend the sides of the arbour by attaching an extra frame as shown.

The extended sides of the set. Note how potted plants provide an established look.

MATERIALS LIST

Item	Material	Length (in mm)	No.
Posts	100 x 100	2200	5
Barge board back / front	150 x 25	3050	1 ea
Barge board ends	150 x 25	1200	2
Rafters	100 x 25	1100	14
Ridge	150 x 25	2800	1
Bottom frame end	50 x 50	450	2
front (short)	50 x 50	650	2
front (long)	50 x 50	2200	1
seat verticals	50 x 50	375	7
Top frame end struts	75 x 38	374	4
back struts	75 x 38	274	3
front (short)	75 x 38	962	2
front (long)	75 x 38	2100	1
back (short)	75 x 38	1000	2
back (long)	75 x 38	2924	1

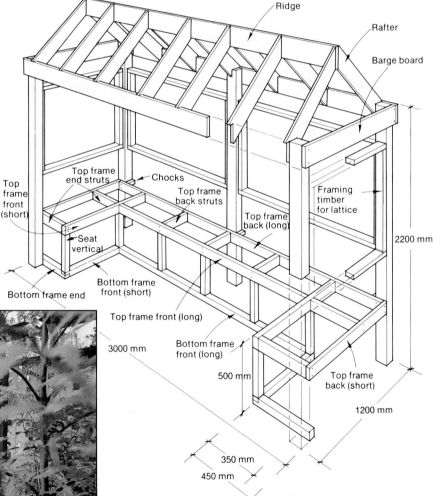

Looking into the arbour.

Other. 38 x 12 mm oregon or similar for seating slats; purchased lattice panels; 75 x 38 mm framing timber; 5 m of 50 x 25 mm timber for seat edging; 4 blocks scrap timber for chocks; 75 mm nails; paint to finish.

9

ROOFED PERGOLA

This fairly lightweight structure creates a lovely halfway point between the inside environment and the open garden. Paving and planting also help to link the pergola with the garden. The post bracket set into concrete is the most permanent and satisfactory way of standing posts.

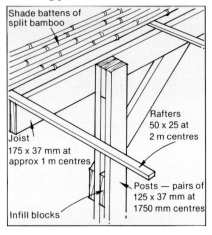

Shade battens of split bamboo

Rafters 50 x 25 at 2 m centres

Joist 175 x 37 mm at approx 1 m centres

Posts — pairs of 125 x 37 mm at 1750 mm centres

Infill blocks

FREESTANDING PERGOLA

A pergola can take the form of a completely freestanding structure like this. By building pairs of columns at the corners, 300 mm apart, and using lattice panels as an infill, you gradually enclose the structure. Be careful not to block it off from the rest of the garden. By screening substantial areas of the walls the structure will become a gazebo or shadehouse.

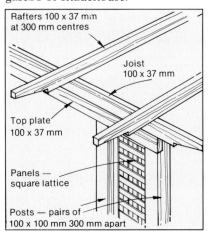

Rafters 100 x 37 mm at 300 mm centres

Joist 100 x 37 mm

Top plate 100 x 37 mm

Panels — square lattice

Posts — pairs of 100 x 100 mm 300 mm apart

BARBECUE AND PAVING

A good barbecue gets the cooking out of the kitchen, liberates the indoor cook and is basic to the all-Australian enjoyment of outdoor living. The barbecue should be located centrally. Halfway between the kitchen and a shady outdoor dining area is a good position.

BUILDING THE BARBECUE

Bricklayers will tell you that this is not a job for amateurs. However, as long as you plan the job well and constantly check the vertical and horizontal levels as you proceed you shouldn't have any trouble.

Choose the bricks carefully. A barbecue is a relatively small item so it doesn't easily take a brick with high contrast markings. The bricks shown here are PGH Bounty sandstock. You will need 300

quality bricks and approximately 70 commons (for fill). To support the hotplate frame have four 75 mm lengths of 25 mm flat steel close at hand.

Plan the size of your barbecue on paper. This one is planned around a prefabricated hotplate and grate combined (from Barbeques Galore in all states). It comes with its own supporting angle iron frame. The whole unit measures 660 x 480 mm. You will have to allow 225 mm brickwork outside that. We had to make some of the mortar joints as wide as 15 mm in order to expand the structure and enable it to accommodate the hotplate unit.

Decide whether you want to include the curved back wall. It involves more cutting of bricks but gives the structure a more interesting appearance.

1. Dig area one brick course down. Set common bricks into a mortar bed.

2. Cover with mortar, smooth over. Add water for bonding of next layer.

3. For the curved back you will have to cut bricks. Use a cold chisel on grass.

4. Set out the first course as shown, filling the wedge-shaped joints with mortar.

5. Check with a spirit level as you proceed.

6. Continue upwards laying bricks over joints and planning for the iron frame.

7. Fill the centre with rubble and cement to make the first platform, seven courses up.

8. Lay double thickness brickwork, using the iron frame to check distance.

9. Cut the bricks neatly on the inside of the curve. These will be visible.

10. Two courses up, set 75 mm lengths of flat steel in the mortar to take the frame.

11. Finish with a row of header bricks to trim and strengthen the structure.

For the laying mortar use white bush sand and off-white cement (five parts sand to one part cement). To each barrow-load of mortar add one capful of plaster sizer. This makes the mortar more workable and allows you to tap the bricks into place. It also makes it unnecessary to work with wet bricks.

When you fill in the central void with rubble or common bricks, you can use washed river sand and gravel and ordinary cement, four parts to one.

The easiest way to finish the mortar joints is to scrape them off flush with the brickwork.

PAVING

Laying pavers dry is the easiest way to achieve a professional finish. It will allow you to 'play' with the bricks, even to start again if you are not satisfied with the result. The principles of paving are shown here on a small area in front of the barbecue. The method is the same for large areas.

Select a paver which is contrasted in colour with other brickwork nearby. These are PGH Amazon pavers, chosen to contrast with the sandy-coloured brickwork. They measure 230 x 115 x 50 mm. You can work out the number you will require by measuring the area you intend to pave.

With dry laying, the job is only as strong as the edges, as these hold all the pavers in place. For this reason the paving should either be laid flush with the finished ground level, or have cement or soil mounded around the edge. Make the outer bricks headers (laid endways) for added strength.

1. Decide on the area to be paved as a multiple of brick size. Dig it level.

2. Lay two level lengths of timber or pipe in sand bed and use to rake the sand level.

3. Lay header bricks along one long and one short edge to plan the whole area.

4. Use timber length, level and mallet to tap the bricks to an even surface.

5. Sweep and hose sand into the joints to compact and set the paving.

When you lay the sand bed, add a thin layer of cement and mix the two lightly with your shovel. Damp the sand and cement slightly before raking level as the photographs indicate. For a large area, screed sand about 2 m at a time and work from the already laid bricks.

When you sweep and hose the job to finish, let the bricks sit for about two hours before scrubbing them clean.

BENCH SEAT AND PERGOLA

Use every opportunity to enhance an outdoor setting. A wall is ideal for a pergola and, if it is blank, you can add a lattice panel above a new garden bench. Unadorned windowsills may be crying out for windowboxes. Make them with 50 x 25 mm frames and lattice panels supported on brackets.

BUILDING THE SEAT

Build the garden bench to the size you prefer. The one illustrated is 2100 mm long to run between two pergola posts. If it's more than 1500 mm, include a seat support across the platform halfway along.

This whole structure is made of 100 x 50 mm preservative-impregnated pine. You can sometimes buy this with a rebate running down its length to take the heavy prefabricated lattice panels. If you are not able to obtain this and you do not have access to a router to make the rebate yourself, you will have to nail strips of 40 x 20 mm timber either side of the lattice panels on the ends and beneath the seat panels on the platform. Make sure the seat panels finish flush with

1. Make the end frames 900 mm high and 600 mm wide. Mitre joints.

2. Cut 450 mm high lattice panels to fit into the slots. Slide them into place.

3. Drill and screw horizontals under the lattice panels to hold them in place.

4. Make the bed platform frame with butt joints to fit between the legs.

5. Insert the lattice seat panel, supported by struts.

6. Drill and screw platform level with lower horizontals in ends.

7. Insert three screws through each leg into the platform.

8. Drill and glue the four large finials or knobs at the corners; finish as desired.

the top of the seat frame.

For benches over 2 m long you will have to make the mattress in two equal lengths of 100 mm-thick foam. Make the bolsters with rolls of similar foam. If you prefer, instead of piping and upholstering both ends of the bolsters and surfaces of the mattress, make the sides longer than necessary and use drawstrings to pull them together on the hidden sides.

MAKING THE PERGOLA

If possible make your pergola a logical extension of your house, a step in the transition from the inside to the outside. Combine all the components to create an enjoyable atmosphere for family and friends.

Dressed oregon is best for the job. Make the posts of 100 x 100 mm and the joists and rafters of 100 x 50 mm. Note that you will have to plan ahead for the whole structure so that you can saw all joints on the ground.

Pictures 2 and 4 show that the front joist extends past the corner post to allow the end rafter to intersect with it.

When you mark out your pergola, work on the basis that the posts be no less than 1.5 m and no more than 2.5 m apart. You should then allow two or three rafters between those that occur at the posts. This is because pergolas are framed structures only and require a reasonable number of components to make them appear substantial.

If you decide not to use our suggestions of slatted barge panels and cut-out corner brackets (see pictures 5 and 6), you should include some other form of trim.

Our posts are trimmed by a chamfer down each corner edge. You can execute it with a plane but an electric router will make the job quicker and more accurate.

1. Set the post brackets into concrete and prop the posts in a vertical position.

2. Lift and bolt the front joist into position. It should overhang the corner post.

3. Position the rafters. Support them in notches cut into a wall plate bolted to the wall.

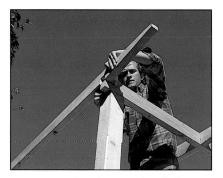

4. Lift the rafters into notches in the front joist and on the outside of the corner posts.

5. Use 150 mm-long slats nailed to lengths of 50 x 50 mm timber. Nail to the posts and joist back.

6. Make 150 x 150 mm corner brackets, 35 mm thick. Drill and jigsaw cut-out patterns.

WINDOW GREENHOUSE

Any sunny window offers a back wall for an easily constructed frame that rests on the sill.

Construct a 50 x 25 mm frame to rest on the sill. Then add the front flap (three strips of old leather belt for hinges and metal mending plates for corners). Build in 300 x 25 mm shelves at varying heights and staple 0.15 mm plastic sheet to the frame. The greenhouse pictured is propped open to allow for watering but is normally open only a few millimetres for air circulation.

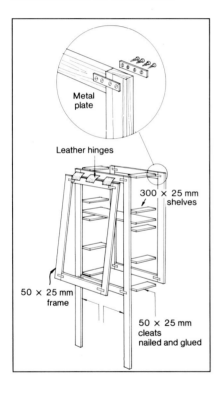

Metal plate

Leather hinges

300 × 25 mm shelves

50 × 25 mm frame

50 × 25 mm cleats nailed and glued

HANGING GARDEN POST

Pretty flowering baskets demand star treatment — build this simple structure to make them the centre of attention. The triangular bracket swings 180° around the post on hinges, enabling the plants to follow the sun.

Cut out all components listed. First, saw and chisel the decorative top to the post, using our picture as a guide. Set a metal post bracket in a semi-dry concrete footing.

Next, assemble the triangular support bracket. Drill and screw the horizontal to the top of the vertical at a 90° angle. Mark points 300 mm along the horizontal and 200 mm down the vertical for the diagonal. Using saw and chisel, cut 25 mm-deep notches at these points to accommodate the diagonal, and angle the ends of the diagonal to fit into them. Skew nail the diagonal in place.

Stand the post and bolt it securely to the post bracket. Position the support bracket 400 mm down from the top of the post and hinge it approximately 150 mm from its top and bottom.

Trim the ends of the two hanger pieces as shown in the picture, and cut a half-lap joint at the centres to

16

allow them to intersect. Screw pieces together. Insert cup hooks at the end of the horizontal, in the centre of the hanger, and underneath the ends of the hanger. Suspend the hanger from the horizontal with a chain.

Now your post is all ready for baskets of trailing flowers and greenery. Suspend them carefully so that they balance each other and hang straight. This post makes a delightful welcome to a garden when placed at a gateway or entrance.

MATERIALS LIST

All components are cut from hardwood			
Item	Material	Length or size (in mm)	No.
Post	100 x 100 mm	2500	1
Vertical	100 x 75 mm	800	1
Horizontal	100 x 75 mm	850	1
Diagonal	100 x 75 mm	650	1
Hanger	75 x 25 mm	700	2

Other. 150 mm coach screws; two 150 mm hinges; cup hooks; chain; post bracket and bolts.

WOODEN WALKWAY

Give old fence palings a new life by converting them to attractive walkways. Timber paving is best suited to low rainfall areas. In wetter climates, keep timber paving out in the open; in constant shade it will develop moss, become slippery and require regular wire brushing to keep its surface safe. Decide on the configuration of the walkway — ours is in off-set rectangular modules and steps down over three levels. Select splinter-free, unwarped palings, cut them to the width of the path and paint each side with a wood preservative such as ⅓ creosote, ⅓ kerosene and ⅓ sump oil. Nail palings to fence rails and position walkways on a bed of material which drains well. Use more rails to define the changes in level and divide garden beds.

GARDENER'S POTTING BENCH

An unsightly array of bags of potting mix and untidy heaps of vacant pots usually signal the average home gardener's workplace for potting up plants. Use an outdoor table to lift the potting procedure off the ground and eliminate backache and you'll have nowhere to rest your cup of tea. The whole process would be much more elegantly accommodated at a potting bench which could be along one side of a greenhouse or conservatory, on one wall of the garage or carport or simply placed against an exterior wall. Although this potting bench is basically a utility area, its component parts are pleasant to look at and with the use of lattice screening the structure could make a handsome addition to the garden landscape. The unit has been designed to hold four bins. With less space, it could be reduced in size. If space is no problem, and potting plants is a popular activity at your house, the bench could be easily lengthened. The wall above the bench could be fitted with hooks, nails and fittings to keep small garden tools in order. To begin, simply read the Materials List and tick the various components off in your mind against the drawing. When you are familiar with the structure, cut out all the components as listed. Follow our step-by-step instructions and photographs for easy assembly. Simple notches and cleats give the structure strength.

CUTTING OUT THE NOTCHES

1. Cut the 250 x 38 mm and 100 x 38 mm notches in the front legs to accommodate the front stretcher and top rail. Note that the leg at the join in the bench top is 100 mm shorter than the other two (the same length as the corner legs) to allow the top stud to rest on it. Locate the stretcher notches between the 100 and 350 mm points up the legs from the bottom and on the front surface. It is easier to cut the notches with a circular saw but a handsaw will do. Make sure the timber is firmly clamped in place if you are using a circular saw.

2. Use a handsaw to square up these cuts and to cut in from the outside.

3. Tidy up the cuts with a rasp. You will need to do this throughout the assembly of the bench to get rid of the stubble or burring caused by the saw.

4. Now cut the large V notches in the front stretcher to hold the bins when tilted forward. Check the drawing carefully to make sure you mark out the lines correctly before cutting. Note that the V notches are 100 mm deep and 475 mm wide. Make sure you allow for the difference in dimensions at the ends which accommodate the corner leg cleats.

5. Once again finish the cuts with a handsaw and trim up with a rasp.

JOINING CLEATS TO CORNER LEGS

6. Mark up the corner leg assemblies, using the leg section detail drawing as a guide. Use the cleat itself as a rule.

7. Glue the cleats to the corner legs, remembering in each instance to which corner the leg belongs. Right and left and front and back positions will make the difference to the position of the cleat on the leg.

1. Cut out notches for stretchers and top rail.

2. Square up and finish notches with handsaw.

3. Rasp out stubble for final trimming of cuts.

4. Saw out the large V cuts in the stretcher.

5. Finish cutting Vs with a handsaw.

6. Mark out position of the leg cleats.

7. Reinforce joints with wood glue.

8. Nail cleats to legs extending 100 mm at top.

9. Lay out front legs to check the sequence.

10. Fix the side stretchers to the back legs.

Check the drawing as you proceed.
8. Nail the cleats in position. The cleats will reinforce the joints between the end top studs and top rails. Also note that the corner legs are only 830 mm long and that the cleats add 100 mm height to the top of the legs.
9. Lay out the front legs in sequence to make sure you are proceeding correctly.

ASSEMBLING THE COMPONENTS

10. Nail the side stretchers to the inside of the back corner legs. These finish flush with the back surface of the legs. To ensure that the joint is 90° use a square.
11. Bore pilot holes in the front stretcher to prevent it splitting when nailing it to the front legs. Use three nails in each joint and reinforce each one with wood glue. Now you have the main components assembled.
12. Assemble the top frame with butt joints. Lay it upside down on the floor and use as the base for assembling the legs. Nail the front legs and already attached front stretcher to the top frame.
13. Attach the side assembly to the front corner legs, gluing and nailing through the side stretcher into the inside of the front leg and then through the front stretcher into the end of the side stretcher. Nail through the back leg cleats into the top frame. At this point sand and rasp all the edges and exposed cuts.
14. Turn the bench up the right way and move it into position. Tap the wall to locate wall studs and mark their position on the inside of the rear top rail. Drill holes through the back rail into the wall studs to take the 125 mm-long 6 mm-diameter screws.

11. Nail front stretcher to front legs.

12. Nail front leg assembly to the top frame.

13. Attach side stretcher to front corner leg.

14. Drill holes through back rail into wall studs.

15. Cut out bench top hatch and fix corner cleats.

16. Nail benches and drop lid in place.

ADDING THE BENCH TOPS

15. Cut out the bench top hatch in bench B using a jigsaw, circular saw or drill and keyhole saw. Nail four 75 mm-long cleats across the corners of the underside to hold the lid in place.

16. Fix bench tops in position. Drop hatch in place and use a screw or screw eye as a knob for lifting.

MATERIALS LIST

Item	Material	Length or size (in mm)	No.
Front legs	100 x 38 mm pine	930	2
		830	1
Front stretcher	250 x 38 mm pine	2690	1
Corner legs	100 x 38 mm pine	830	4
Corner leg cleats	38 x 38 mm pine	580	4
Side stretchers	250 x 38 mm pine	712	2
Front / rear top rails	100 x 38 mm pine	2766	1 ea
Top studs	100 x 38 mm pine	674	3
Top A	18 mm form ply	2046 x 750	1
Top B	18 mm form ply	750 x 720	1
Cut-out cleats	25 x 12 mm pine	75	4

Other. 125 mm-long 6 mm-dia screws; 75, 50 and 35 mm jolt-head nails; wood glue.

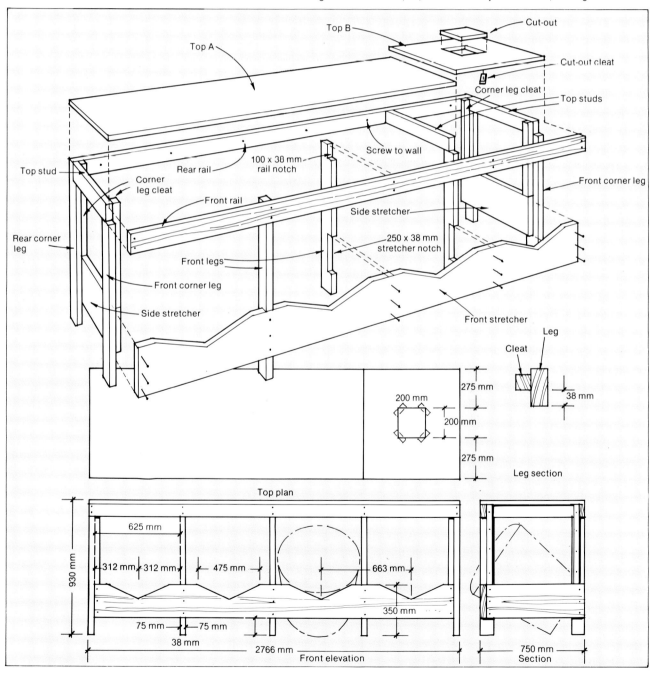

Top B

Cut-out

Top A

Cut-out cleat

Corner leg cleat

Top studs

Screw to wall

Top stud

Rear rail

100 x 38 mm rail notch

Front corner leg

Corner leg cleat

Front rail

Side stretcher

Rear corner leg

250 x 38 mm stretcher notch

Front legs

Front corner leg

Side stretcher

Front stretcher

Leg

Cleat

275 mm

200 mm

200 mm

38 mm

275 mm

Leg section

Top plan

930 mm

625 mm

312 mm   312 mm   475 mm   663 mm

350 mm

75 mm   75 mm

38 mm

2766 mm

Front elevation

750 mm

Section

21

STORAGE

A PLACE FOR EVERYTHING

Too many possessions and not enough space for storage? It is a common problem nowadays but one which did not really trouble our ancestors. Excess of household goods and personal possessions is characteristic of a rich modern society. In countries where accommodation is scarce and wages are low, an odd cupboard and a couple of shelves most probably cope with the lot. But in privileged societies such as ours, homemakers are constantly crying out for more storage of one kind or another. A house without a garage means not so much a threat to the shine on the car as a sorry lack of somewhere to store skis, sailboards, surfboards and unwieldy pieces of equipment like trampolines when not in use.

Before installing shelves and cupboards on every spare wall it is a good idea to take stock of all the possessions in a house and classify them. A good test of an item's worth is to determine whether or not it has been used in the last 12 months. Items which fail should be cast out. There are, however, some very important things such as Christmas decorations which only surface annually. Being, for the most part, delicate and brittle, they need protective but not particularly handy storage. Polystyrene fruit boxes, although bulky, are ideal and they can be placed on the highest shelf or at the bottom of a trunk. Categorise things to be stored as 'everyday', 'frequent', 'once in a while' and 'seldom' and store accordingly.

'Seldoms' should go in lightweight, lidded boxes and be put in difficult-to-reach-without-a-ladder places. In old houses with high ceilings, there is plenty of this stowage space overhead which can be used with attractively edged shelves supported securely by strong brackets. (A piece of bevelled timber fixed to the edge of a particle board shelf will give the plank strength as well as an attractive, solid appearance.)

'Everydays' such as crockery, cutlery and glassware in constant use can be exposed on shelves and racks because they will never be still long enough to gather dust. It is the 'frequents' and 'once in a whiles' (best dinner services, evening clothes and fondue sets) which complicate storage and give rise to the need for protection from household fallout and the sands of time.

Sophisticated and relatively inexpensive storage systems for clothing, books and sound equipment can be bought 'off the shelf', brought home and assembled without too much fuss and distress. But occasions arise when there is a need for a supplement to existing storage — a shoe rack, a hall stand or a corner unit — which will set the handy person thinking of a visit to the timber yard, then a quick spin around the hardware shop and an enjoyable weekend in the workshop.

A corner storage unit providing useful space in a kitchen (see page 35)

BEDROOM CLOTHES RACK

This practical and stylish rack will give you all the clothes storage you need without the expense and trouble of constructing built-ins.

Following the materials list below, cut the components as you proceed. Start by joining feet to bottom horizontal using half-lap joints (see diagram). Drill and screw through the joints and into the bottom of the posts, using two screws for each joint. To fit the feet braces, cut 45° angles at either end and saw out a 37 x 35 mm section at the top end to enable them to fit around the post. Screw them together at the top as well as to the post and the foot.

Mitre ends of inner braces and screw in place. Screw the central post in place through bottom of

The three bottom braces hold the posts upright. Shelf braces allow heavy suitcases to be up out of the way. Add diagonal dowel clothes pegs if you require them.

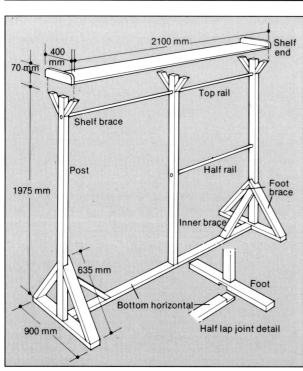

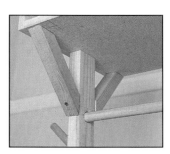

MATERIALS LIST

Item	Material	Length or size (in mm)	No.
Posts	70 x 37 mm pine	1975	3
Bottom horizontal	70 x 37 mm pine	2100	1
Feet	70 x 37 mm pine	900	2
Feet braces	70 x 37 mm pine	635	4
Inner braces	70 x 37 mm pine	625	2
Shelf	19 mm edged particle board	2100 x 400	1
Shelf braces	37 x 37 mm pine	525	6
Shelf ends	70 x 19 mm pine	400	2
Top rail	25 mm dowel	2063	1
Half rail	25 mm dowel	1031	1

Other. 40 mm and 60 mm countersunk screws; wood filler.

horizontal. Glue and screw shelf ends to the shelf. Screw through the shelf into the top of the end posts, remembering to face the finished timber edge of the shelf to the front.

Drill holes in posts to take dowel rails; position the top dowel 150 mm below the shelf and the half rail 900 mm up from the floor. Drill holes slightly larger than the dowels, noting that you should drill only halfway into outer posts to accommodate ends of dowels. Drill and screw into the dowel ends through the posts.

Fit and screw the shelf braces in place and fill and sand all screw· holes. Paint if required.

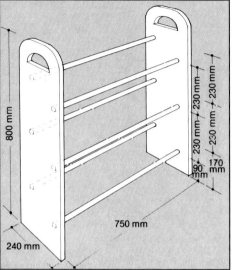

SENSIBLE SHOE RACK

If your clothes storage is open, make a display of your footwear. This rack is also small enough to tuck behind cupboard doors or sit in front of your clothes rack. Mark out the side shapes on 240 x 19 mm pine; also mark the position of the six 25 mm dowels 40 mm in from the edges. Then drill and jigsaw the hand grip cut-outs towards the top, using the drawing as a guide. All you then have to do is drill, glue and screw the structure together.

SMART STORAGE FOR A HALLWAY

These bright ideas provide valuable extra storage near the door.

In most homes storage space is at a premium, so a hallway corner like this is a welcome bonus. Bring it to life with stylish and functional fittings, and you'll have a practical area for storing bulky outdoor gear.

A large cupboard is invaluable for keeping sweaters handy. A couple of pine boxes can be transformed into a cabinet with the addition of a quartet of glass-fronted doors. Place the piece on a plinth of pine planking and paint the whole unit in different shades.

If you can find some chrome-coated pipes or other heavy duty rods, you've the basis for a novel coat rack. Secure the bars to a piece of particle board and mount it at cabinet-top level to keep coats and jackets well out of the way.

The shoe stand is made using a similar technique but this time

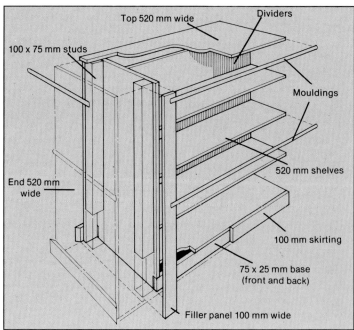

Top 520 mm wide

Dividers

100 x 75 mm studs

Mouldings

520 mm shelves

End 520 mm wide

100 mm skirting

75 x 25 mm base (front and back)

Filler panel 100 mm wide

upside down, with a metal grille incorporated in a frame of particle board. This smart accessory should inspire the family to keep its shoes in one place!

Finish off the brightened-up corner with a fun umbrella stand. Cut out a cat, or any pet you fancy, from a sheet of plywood. Paint realistically and place on guard in front of your umbrellas.

FREESTANDING SHELVING

• Try to replicate details in different situations to reduce the number of conflicting elements in an interior. In this situation, the shelving end becomes a section of wall built in timber stud construction, to echo the room divider.

• To do this, the outside surface of the shelving end wall must be fixed in place last to allow you to drill and screw through the timber frame into the edge of the shelves.

• This enables the shelves to be supported without unsightly cleats beneath their ends.

• Use the same semicircular moulding on the edge of the shelves. Where the shelves occur close together, as in the case of book storage, add the moulding detail on alternate shelves so that the distance between the wall shadow lines remains constant throughout the room.

COAT AND CASE RACK

A slatted shelf with pegs for coats and umbrellas will clear the floor of bags and rainwear at the front door. You need 50 x 25 mm DAR timber, 32 x 25 mm timber scraps; 19 mm dowel; 12 mm DAR timber scraps; wood screws.

Shelf. Use 50 x 25 mm timber for shelf supports and braces and half-lap all joints as shown. Separate each assembly with pieces of 32 x 25 mm timber; glue and clamp. When the glue has dried, nail and glue seven 1000 mm-long pieces of 50 x 25 mm timber to the top, leaving about 9 mm between each piece. To attach the unit to the wall, screw two metal hanging brackets to the back of the shelf support separators. Also screw to the wall through spacers as shown.

Coat rack. Drill five 19 mm-diameter holes in the 100 x 25 mm coat rack. Insert 75 mm lengths of dowel with 30 mm diameter rounds cut from 12 mm scrap timber screwed to one end. Glue and screw the rack to the shelf supports using two 38 mm x 10 gauge countersunk wood screws at each joint.

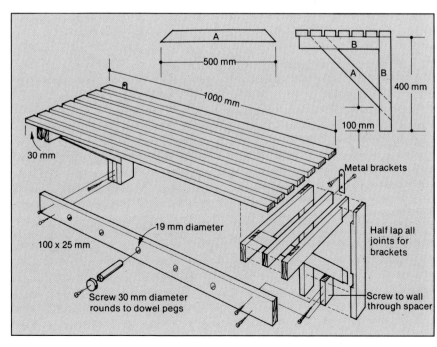

CORNER CABINET

The triangular form of the cabinet results in slight variations in dimensions; custom-fit components to size as you proceed.

Start by assembling the three legs and two sides. We cut the rear leg to a triangular section but if that is too difficult use the 50 x 50 mm square section of timber and adapt the shelves, top and bottom to fit around it. Cut 12 x 12 mm rebates in the outside edge of the front legs to take the sides. Assemble with glue and screws. Note detail of the leg section which shows how to build up an edge from which to hinge the doors later. Fix the hingeing battens in place and bevel off the edge (see diagram).

Measure and cut the bottom piece, making it about 10 mm shallower at the front to allow for the 7 mm-thick trim. Glue and nail it in position through sides and legs. Measure and cut the three shelves and top of cabinet. Screw in place. Nail the bottom shelf trim in place.

Make the two door frames to size, checking as you go. If you do not have the facilities for making a rebate to take the glass, tack glazing beading either side of the glass along the inside edge of the frame. Drill, glue and dowel-peg the door frames together. Fix the doors in place with hinges; add ball catches at top and bottom. Screw on knobs.

Cut the curved pediment to shape as shown. Angle off the ends of the top rail and screw it to top and legs as in the diagram. Screw the pediment to the top rail. For extra strength, screw the pediment support through back of pediment and into the top rail.

Use dowel pegs to fix the curved trims to the top of the front legs. Undercoat and finish with semi-gloss paint, using our picture as a guide. Line the inside of the cabinet walls with felt.

MATERIALS LIST

Item	Material	Length or size (in mm)	No.
Sides	12 mm ply	1290 x 675	2
Shelves	12 mm ply	Cut as diagram	3
Top/bottom	12 mm ply	Cut as diagram	2
Curved pediment	18 mm ply	770 x 500	1
Pediment support	50 x 50mm softwood	770	1
Rear leg	50 x 50 mm softwood	1790	1
Front legs	140 x 20 mm softwood	1790	2
Top rail	100 x 50 mm softwood	900	1
Bottom trim	30 x 7 mm softwood	770	1
Leg top trim	75 x 18 mm softwood	130	2
Door sides	45 x 30 mm softwood	1290	4
Door tops/bottoms	45 x 30 mm softwood	290	4
Hingeing battens	45 x 20 mm softwood	1290	2

Other. white glue: 40 mm countersunk screws; 38 mm nails; dowels; 75 mm brass butt hinges; ball catches and door knobs; paint; felt.
Note. All timber measurements are finished (dressed) sizes.

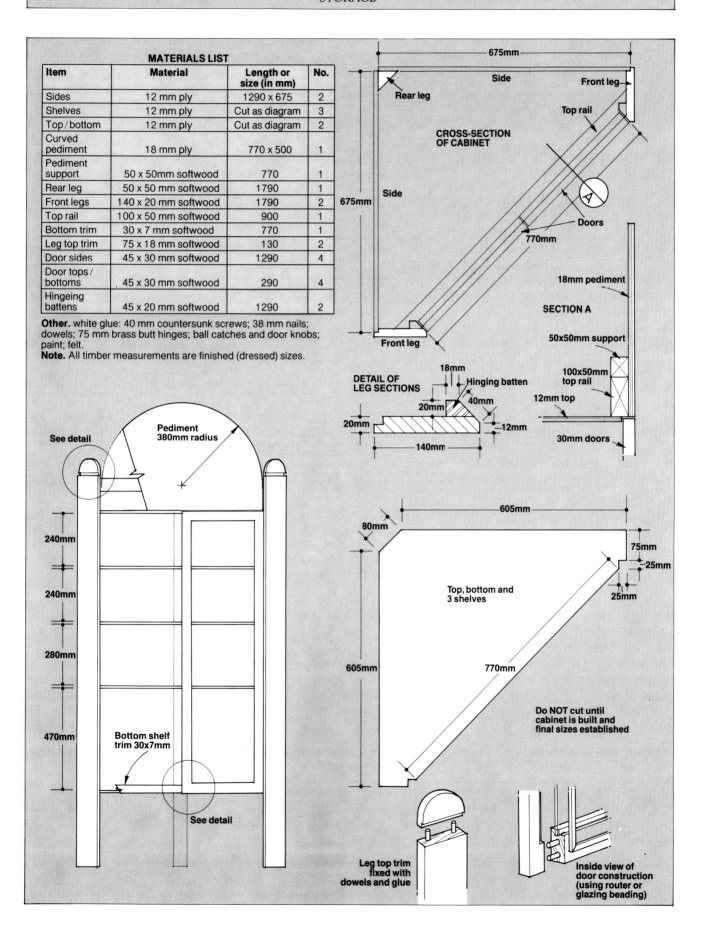

CROSS-SECTION OF CABINET

675mm

Side

Rear leg

Front leg

Top rail

675mm

Side

Doors

770mm

Front leg

18mm pediment

SECTION A

50x50mm support

100x50mm top rail

12mm top

30mm doors

DETAIL OF LEG SECTIONS

18mm

Hinging batten

40mm

20mm

20mm

12mm

140mm

See detail

Pediment 380mm radius

240mm

240mm

280mm

470mm

Bottom shelf trim 30x7mm

See detail

80mm

605mm

75mm

25mm

25mm

Top, bottom and 3 shelves

605mm

770mm

Do NOT cut until cabinet is built and final sizes established

Leg top trim fixed with dowels and glue

Inside view of door construction (using router or glazing beading)

TIE AND BELT RACK

Backs of doors are very useful. Store all your scarves, belts and ties on these handy homemade rails. This double dowel keeps the items from sliding off. Make the top rail from 12 mm dowel and the bottom from 6 mm dowel and position them about 10 mm apart. Use our picture as a guide for the shape of the brackets, making them from 19 mm-thick timber. Drill holes halfway through to hold the ends of the dowels. Make sure part of the bracket is thin enough to enable you to drill and screw it in place.

SPACE-SAVING SHOE SHELVES

Narrow shelving for shoes can sit in front of the washing machine. The shelves are only 250 mm deep and because they are supported by tracks and brackets, they can easily be lifted out if the machine needs attention. Give ordinary plastic-laminated particle board an extra trim by framing it with 12 x 12 mm pine.

WHEEL-ABOUT STORAGE SCREEN

Keep all your sewing and hobby gear neat and tidy in this super storage system. Make frames and shelves from 90 x 19 mm finished pine backed with 13 mm particle board. Join the panels with 100 mm butt hinges. Hold everything in place with expanding curtain wire, cup hooks and panel pins, and roll it about on castors.

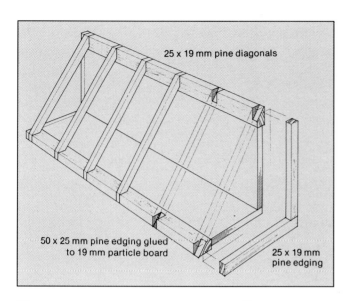

25 x 19 mm pine diagonals

50 x 25 mm pine edging glued to 19 mm particle board

25 x 19 mm pine edging

PINE UMBRELLA STAND

This hall unit is made from two 230 mm boxes of 25 x 100 mm pine. The lower box has a 3 mm hardboard bottom. Two crossed 6 mm rods divide each box. Connect the top and bottom with two 600 mm lengths of 25 x 50 mm pine. Sand and apply polyurethane.

RECORD STORAGE

Records will stay safely stacked in this felt-lined storage rack. You'll find you can make it in record time, too, from particle board and pine. You will need some 19 mm particle board; 50 x 25 mm and 25 x 19 mm pine; felt.

Cut back and base pieces 650 x 250 mm from particle board. Glue 50 x 25 pine edging to one long side

of each piece, and cut six equally spaced slots in the edgings for the diagonals. Nail and glue back and base together. Line particle board surfaces with felt, using a thin coat of PVA glue. When dry, glue 25 x 19 diagonals in the slots; cut the ends flush to edges. Edge the particle board ends with 25 x 19. Finish off by rounding the corners with a sander.

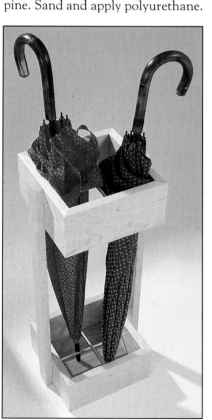

SHOW-OFF GLASSWARE RACK

Cut 100 x 25 mm pine slats into five 450 mm lengths. Make a 400 mm square frame from 50 x 25 mm pine.

So that glasses will slide, screw slats to the frame from above using 50 mm woodscrews, and glue and screw two 25 x 25 mm spacers between each slat and the frame. Sand and stain.

CABINET IN FOUR DIFFERENT STYLES

The basic structure of this versatile unit can be adapted to suit any style of room.

Here's a building project on which you can really use your imagination. We give you the simple construction method but after that you can use your design skills to give the cupboard an individual touch. The pictures of four different decorative schemes demonstrate structural variations as well as alternative uses and finishing treatments, but these are only suggestions. You may be able to come up with more innovative designs. Follow the step-by-step diagrams and pictures to build the basic structure, then fill the edges and apply the undercoat. Sit the shape in your room and decide how to finish it.

1. Cut out the three 18 mm particle board components to the dimensions shown on our drawing. Using a square and clamp, glue and screw the back to the rear edges of the top and bottom. You can use 50 mm particle board screws for the job but 50 mm furniture connectors tightened with an Allen key, which you should buy in the correct size along with the connectors, are guaranteed not to split the board.

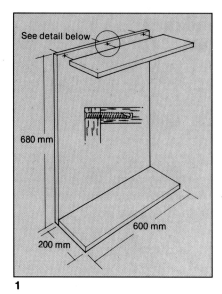

1

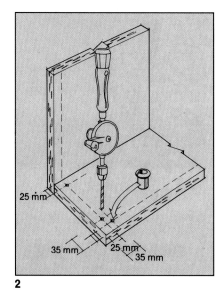

3

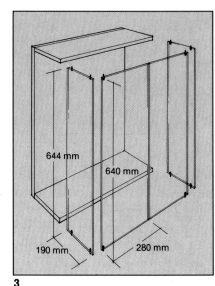

2

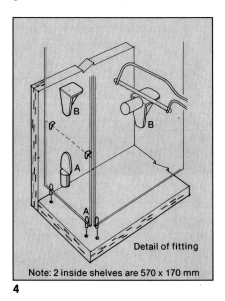

Detail of fitting

Note: 2 inside shelves are 570 x 170 mm

4

2. Drill 5 mm holes in the top and bottom at the points indicated on the diagram. The two at the side are for the spoon-shaped shelf supports which will support the fixed side sheets of glass. The single holes at the front of each corner will take the plastic cup fittings into which the pivoting supports will sit. Paint, paper, lacquer or veneer the surfaces.

3. Now set the shelf supports in place and assemble with cardboard instead of glass components. Do this for the sides and shelves. Check that the doors do not rub against the sides when opened.

Take the cardboard shapes to your glazier to have the glass cut and bevelled to size. Use epoxy resin to fix the glass, leaving door flanges to pivot in their cups.

4. To set the shelves in place use plug-in right-angled shelf supports. Use a small hacksaw to remove the flange which would normally fit into the timber vertical of a shelving unit. This will give you a flat surface to glue to the inside of the glass sides to rest the shelves on. Glue small handles to the bottom of the glass doors. Screw through the back into your wall.

CONTEMPORARY

To accentuate the unsupported glass corners of your wall cupboard, glue strips of 30 x 10 mm timber down the edges of the two doors and paint them and the cabinet side edges in the same shade. This gives the unit a sharp, sleek appearance. If the door knobs are to be screwed, position them first. Paint the back of the glass behind to conceal the glue or fix similar timber pieces on the inside surface, leaving gaps to avoid the shelf edges.

TRADITIONAL

Wallpaper all the particle board surfaces to match your room and cover all the glass edges with timber strips, to make your cabinet more suited to the traditionally decorated home. Glue and tack the strips to the edges of the particle board and use epoxy glue to fix the horizontal strips to the outside of the doors and sides hiding the edges of the shelves.

ARCHITECTURAL

Add a triangular pediment to the top by screwing up into its edge through the cabinet top. Fix a podium base to the bottom, 25 mm wider at the sides and front. For a whimsical touch, paper the pediment in a chequerboard pattern. For maximum effect you could add a battery clock with hands only showing at the front. Complete the architectural theme with a small flag at the apex.

BRIGHT

Even in its simplest form, your wall cupboard can make a big impression. Just by painting it one bright colour it becomes perfect for a child's room. Store equally bright items in it to give a graphic and up-to-the-minute accent. You might like to paint each of the three components a different primary colour or go further with bold abstract designs. Play with it — you can always repaint if you don't like the result.

CORNER STORAGE UNIT

Cut out all components listed. Assemble the 10 shelf structures by screwing evenly spaced slats to supports. Note that all the 262 mm ends fit between the shelf supports. Screw three posts to the long shelves and four to the shorter ones.

The shorter shelves, which have nine slats, carry the towel rails, so supports extend 60 mm past the posts to accommodate them. Screw the two sections together through the supports and into the posts. Screw dowel rails in place. The back slats fit behind the rear corner post and in front of the other two rear posts.

MATERIALS LIST

Item	Material	Length (in mm)	No.
Posts	40 x 19 mm pine	2030	7
Shelf supports	40 x 19 mm pine	745	10
		660	10
Shelf ends	40 x 19 mm pine	262	10
Shelf slats	40 x 19 mm pine	300	100
Back slats	40 x 19 mm pine	920	7
Towel rails	13 mm dowel	262	5

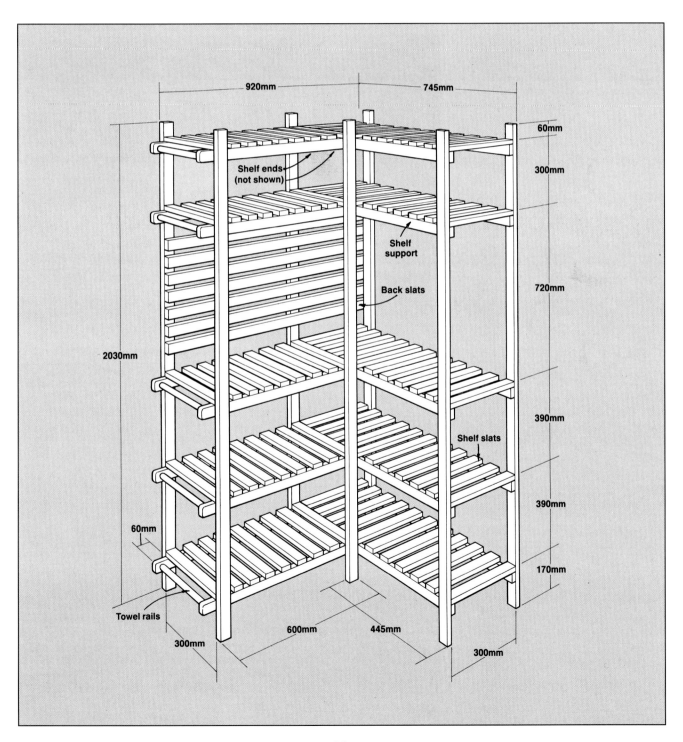

35

WINDOWS

THE LINK BETWEEN HOUSE AND GARDEN

Windows give homes personality. But as well as endowing interiors and exteriors with memorable impact, windows themselves can possess personality. When small, they can imply secrecy, intimacy, protection. Conversely, they are extrovert, welcoming, all-embracing when large. Medium-sized, they are just right. If a window is less than perfectly proportioned, its decorative (and frequently functional) window treatment can create an illusion which will solve the proportion problem and promote the window from being a mere donor of light and fresh air to a focus for beauty. Curtains and blinds can do much to enhance a window but a little deft cabinet-making will do even more. Additions and alterations to windows can make an incredible difference to a room and to the whole house.

If windows are the eyes of a building, then surely windowboxes are the alluring eye make-up. Previously the preserve of picturesque postcards of quaint villages and sophisticated ancient apartments of Europe, windowboxes have become more and more popular and are now quite well established all over the world. A greater understanding of the care of plants in troughs and pots combined with the knowledge of correct and safe support of windowboxes have made way for the unprecedented spread of this enchanting form of indoor/outdoor decorating and gardening. There is a general consensus that windowboxes are a delight to behold, from both sides of the glass.

Another idea is to have your windows growing out into the garden; they are given sides, a base and a raked top and pushed beyond the boundaries of the wall to create miniature conservatories or glasshouses. In America, these expanded windows are called 'bump-outs', but whatever the term, the concept is brilliant and it is a wonderful way of adding extra light and an unprecedented feeling of space to a dark and undersized room.

A window enhanced by a custom-made windowbox full of flowers (see page 38)

SPECTACULAR WINDOWBOXES

Any window can earn windowbox status. But a windowbox only looks right if it relates to the window in colour, style and size.

The size of your windowbox will be partly dictated by the size of the long narrow polystyrene planters which make the best liners for the timber structure. These come in lengths of 600 mm and 900 mm and are 220 mm wide and 160 mm deep. Use 190 x 19 mm dressed oregon for the sides and ends and make the ends 230 mm wide. Use simple butt joints at the corners, and glue and nail back and front to edges of ends.

Fix your windowbox to the wall with diagonally braced steel angle brackets; use extra large ones if you have to sit the bracket under the windowsill.

Give the box extra style by painting it in an attractive colour scheme or by adding a front trim of mitred timber moulding, as shown on page 36.

You can add a touch of real whimsy by making the geese shown in the top picture. Enlarge them from the graph below and, using a fretsaw, cut them out of 6 mm plywood. Fill the edges, sand, undercoat and paint in the features. Nail to blocks and sit them on your windowsill.

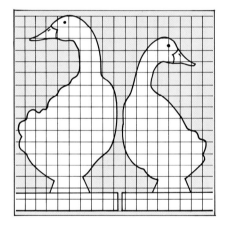

1. Nail 12 x 12 mm or similar timber around the inside bottom edge of the box. This will support the base, which you can cut from plywood or leftover oregon. Glue in, or simply sit the base in place so you can remove it when necessary.

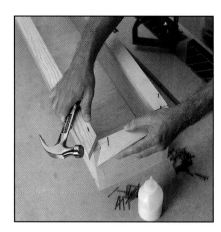

2. Add a top edging trim of 35 x 19 mm timber. For a professional touch, mitre the front two corners but, if you are not up to that, simply butt-join them and fill and sand the edges carefully.

3. For sheer fancy, finish the top edge with an 18 mm scotia trim. It will fit neatly beneath the lip of the 35 x 19 mm edging and you can easily make acceptable mitres in it using a fretsaw and lots of wood filler. Tack and glue it in place.

WINDOWBOXES TO FIT ANY WINDOWSILL

Windowsills vary with different types of housing construction. First, decide whether you want the top of the windowbox to sit level with the sill, below it or above it. Second, using the drawings as a guide, determine a suitable fixing method, depending on the fabric of your walls and the extent to which your windowsill projects. Build the windowbox casing from exterior grade ply. Make it to hold polystyrene troughs which you may then insert and remove for maintenance. If you find the exterior of the ply box too plain, clad it with lattice, shingles, coverstrip layers or weatherboards or drill and fretsaw patterns into the ply itself. Include drainage holes in the bottom of the box. After you have decorated the front of the box, cover the top edge with a 38 x 20 mm timber capping.

Where you have a wide timber windowsill, you may have to fix the back of the box to the edge of the sill. Less stress will be placed on the supporting brackets, so 70 mm-deep shaped timber supports fixed to a wall batten the length of the box will be sufficient.

If your windowsill does not protrude past the wall you can use part of it to take some of the windowbox weight. This will allow shorter brackets. Make them from 35 mm-thick solid timber, and shape as desired. Use expanding bolts to fix them to the brickwork.

Timber brackets that you make yourself will be more conspicuous. You should make them 250 mm wide and at least 300 to 350 mm deep. You will have to notch the diagonals into both the horizontal and vertical pieces for strength. These will allow your box to sit out from the wall.

Pressed metal brackets come in a variety of lengths and sizes. They are ideal if your windowsill does not cantilever too far out from the wall, so that only minimum stress is placed on the brackets. This type of bracket is easily fixed to timber-clad and timber-framed walls.

Heavy steel brackets have a twisted diagonal strut which gives them extra strength. They are available in sizes up to 340 mm in width and are the simplest method of supporting items of such weight. Sloped brick sills vary in width so most weight may be on the end of the brackets.

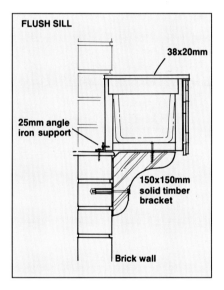

FLUSH SILL

38x20mm

25mm angle iron support

150x150mm solid timber bracket

Brick wall

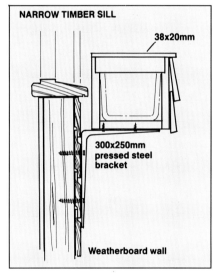

NARROW TIMBER SILL

38x20mm

300x250mm pressed steel bracket

Weatherboard wall

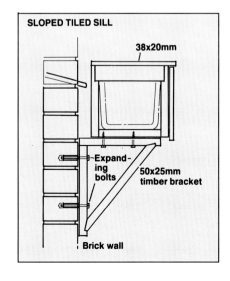

WIDE TIMBER SILL

Screw to sill through back of box

38x20mm

Plywood box and bracket

50x25mm batten

Compressed cement sheet wall lining

SLOPED TILED SILL

38x20mm

Expand-ing bolts

50x25mm timber bracket

Brick wall

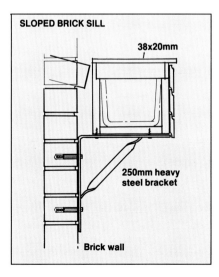

SLOPED BRICK SILL

38x20mm

250mm heavy steel bracket

Brick wall

BUMP-OUT WINDOW

Unless you're an experienced handyperson, this project may be rather ambitious. You can, however, use it to inspire your builder to be adventurous. A bump-out window will give any room an extra dimension as well as being a cosy suntrap and a way of bringing the outside into your home.

Before you begin, decide whether you will fit your bump-out structure with custom-made windows or standard-sized aluminium-framed ones. Check the actual opening size required for each window sash and the standard heights available.

For the window pictured, the sliding side windows were custom-made to a non-standard width of 350 mm and a standard height of 1030 mm.

BUILDING POINTERS

Use dressed oregon or cedar for the framework and follow the drawing as a basic construction guide.

Note that the inside end of the studs for the bump-out floor must be firmly anchored to the wall's timber frame. This will hold the cantilevered floor firm and counteract the weight of the entire structure, making the bricks become the fulcrum on which the floor studs rest.

The floor, of 12 mm ply, should be no deeper than three times the width of the wall.

Note the three-way joint used where horizontal and verticals meet at the junction of the sloping roof.

Fit the window frames according to the manufacturer's specifications. The large front window is fixed glass. This could be an aluminium window sash or simply a sheet of glass sandwiched between strips of beading fixed to the bump-out frame.

Where the sloping sheet of glass that forms the roof of the bump-out

meets the horizontal framing component, it should be allowed to overhang by about 50 mm.

Be sure to use a silicon-based sealer on all joints, especially where the glass and timber meet. It is also vital to fix flashing at the junction between the house wall and bump-out roof.

This kind of window alteration is marvellous when a room suffers from a deficiency of natural light. If a window opens into a light well

where an extension would be out of the question, a bump-out can greatly expand the area of glass and its deep shelf/sill is the perfect stage for a pretty array of plants. For the maximum light boost, paint the wood in white full gloss and house your pots in pale containers. Or opt for clear-finished timber as in our picture.

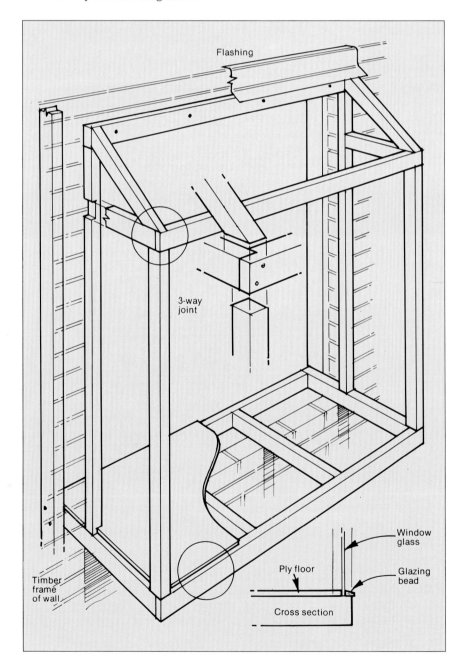

KITCHENS & BATHROOMS

EFFICIENCY AT THE HUB OF THE HOME

Kitchens and bathrooms, even when they are at the hypothetical stage, generate enormous interest among home owners and when the home renovating dollars do start flowing, it is the kitchen and bathroom where most of the money is spent. A wave-the-wand dream kitchen or bathroom, expertly planned on paper and then quickly translated into reality by teams of polite and efficient tradespeople (who have preferably taken vows of silence and have also had their transistor radios confiscated) is without doubt highly desirable.

There is no denying the elegance, efficiency and broad choice of colour in materials like high gloss polyurethane — a mirror-like finish for up-market cupboard and drawer fronts — which is the preserve of sophisticated machinery and controlled factory conditions and definitely not within the equipment and skill limitations of the average handyperson. Or the ease and convenience of nylon runners, especially on deep saucepan and cookware drawers, which glide smoothly with the lightest touch and always stop in time. Nevertheless, furniture, fittings and accessories, made in the workshop, can do a marvellous job of thriftily extending the useful and decorative life of existing kitchens and bathrooms.

Old-fashioned plate racks are a rarity in professionally installed plastic laminate kitchens. But they look good and will quickly earn their keep as hard-working display and storage, ideally suited to the contemporary kitchen's work plan. Shelving spanning a gap between two walls can be a bonus for aesthetics as well as fulfilling the need for extra storage space in the kitchen or bathroom.

Any item built for the kitchen or bathroom should have a water- and grease-proof finish and should preferably be made from material which will not be damaged by an occasional sink or bath overflow.

The kitchen in particular has an atmosphere in which dust and grease residue are generated. With this in mind, plan open storage sensibly and only store constantly used items on exposed shelves and racks.

A timber plate rack with lots of room for crockery (see page 48)

FRAME-UP FOR SAUCEPANS

Try the hanging method for storing pots and pans. This simple timber frame is ideal for fixing into a spare corner close to the stove, or you can hang it from the ceiling. First work out the size you want; the one illustrated is about 1000 mm long by 450 mm deep. Cut 100 x 50 mm dressed oregon to size, mitre and join the corners with glue and two 100 mm-long dowels sanded flush with the surface. Screw in hooks for hanging pots. Fix to the walls using appropriate fasteners, or suspend on chains from a large cuphook screwed into a ceiling joist. Keep lids under control with a length of rope knotted around dowels partially driven into the wall.

ORDERLY CUTLERY DRAWER

Put an end to the lucky-dip system in your cutlery drawer with simple dowel dividers, left. Spacing and layout will depend on the dimensions of your knives, forks and spoons, the quantity to be stored and the size and shape of the drawer. We used 32 mm dowel for spacers, and 32 mm and 25 mm dowel for stops. Cut dowel into 60 mm lengths and sand tops smooth. Using a pencil, mark dowel positions on inside drawer bottom and glue the lengths in place. When glue is dry, screw from the underside of drawer for extra strength.

KNIFE DRAWER WITH TIMBER BLOCKS

A random jumble of knives in a drawer is unsafe and inefficient. Unrestrained blades become blunt as they scrape against one another but never blunt enough to remove the risk of injury to the hand of the

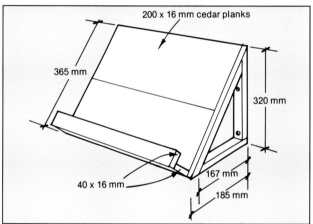

200 x 16 mm cedar planks

365 mm

320 mm

167 mm

40 x 16 mm

185 mm

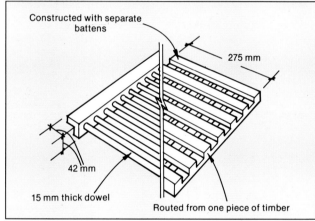

Constructed with separate battens

275 mm

42 mm

15 mm thick dowel

Routed from one piece of timber

busy cook when grappling for a knife. If you prefer the hide-away system to parading your sharpest implements in a wooden block or on a wall-mounted magnetised bar, one solution is to modify an existing drawer with timber insets, as shown below left. Decide on a mean length for your knife-blades and cut the required number of pieces from 38 x 50 mm pine. Glue them to the drawer bottom with fine spacing for blades. (Alternatively, grooves can be cut from one solid timber block if you have an adjustable-depth machine saw.) Glue small 25 mm-thick blocks to support knife handles where necessary.

LECTERN

Keep your favourite cooking references closer to eye level, off valuable bench space and out of the kitchen chaos. This simple wall-mounted lectern solves all the problems.

Use 38 x 16 mm cedar or similar to make the two triangular supports. Make them to the dimensions shown on diagram to allow the book to sit at approximately 60° to the horizontal. Make the sloped surface with timber planks and the bottom sill and lip from 40 x 16 mm timber. Use 30 mm screws and nails to assemble the structure.

HEAT TRIVETS

For the larger dowelled trivet you can use your router to make the L-shaped side/leg components out of 42 mm-square timber or build them up by screwing 19 x 19 mm strips to the underside of the finished structure. Use 300 x 15 mm lengths of dowel. You will require 12 placed at 30 mm centres. Drill 15 mm diameter holes for a neat fit and glue the structure as you proceed.

You can also use a router to make the smaller stand from one block of 30 mm-thick timber or simply nail a number of 15 x 15 mm slats across one another at 30 mm centres.

ATTACHMENT HOLDER

With the increasing number of essential kitchen gadgets it is wise to set a section of your bench space aside as a special appliance centre. It should have sufficient power outlets and enough space to allow the various machines to remain in position.

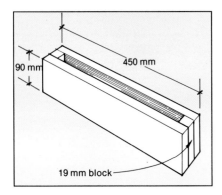

Keep the space clear by having food processor blades and discs close at hand but off the surfaces. Line up the various attachments you wish to accommodate and work out the amount of storage you will require. Cut two 90 x 19 mm or similar lengths of timber (ours are 450 mm long). Screw one to the wall first and then screw or nail 19 mm-thick blocks between it and the outer piece of similar length.

CUTLERY CADDY AND JARS

Cut three long oval pieces from 150 x 25 mm pine and cut three large holes in two of the pieces. Separate these with two uprights of glued 13 mm dowel and glue the third piece to the base. For the matching lids, use 12 mm pine (finished size) and cut two circles 10 mm larger than the diameter of the jar lid. Then trace around lid on one circle and cut out the centre (the lid shape). Glue circle and ring together and screw lid inside ring.

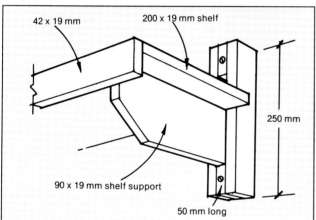

42 x 19 mm
200 x 19 mm shelf
250 mm
90 x 19 mm shelf support
50 mm long

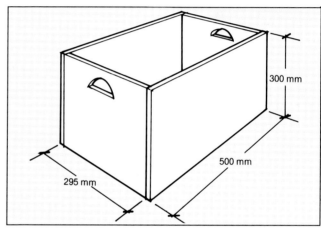

300 mm
500 mm
295 mm

KITCHEN SHELVING

You can build simple storage yourself at a fraction of the cost of factory-made fittings. Open shelves in the kitchen can make your kitchen tidier and more efficient as well as enabling you to make a display of your kitchenware. This shelving system is basic but strong enough to accommodate all your china and jars of cooking ingredients.

To make the brackets, sandwich the 240 mm-long 90 x 19 mm horizontal shelf supports between two 250 mm lengths of vertical 42 x 19 mm timber. Shape the bottom corner as in the diagram.

Fix 50 mm-long blocks between the two verticals and nail the whole bracket together with 35 mm-long jolt-head nails.

To join the horizontal and vertical components, position nails diagonally to each other to counteract the cantilevering force. Use 70 mm countersunk screws to fix the brackets to the wall. Edge the front of the shelf with 42 x 19 mm timber and simply sit the shelf in place.

STORAGE BOX

Deep bins like these are an inexpensive alternative to cupboard doors and drawers.

The boxes pictured were made to suit the dimensions of the shelves so adjust your measurements if necessary, using ours as a guide. Use 9 or 12 mm thick ply for the job. The important factors are that the bins are deep and large enough to allow saucepans, baking dishes, colanders and mixing bowls to fit easily inside. Ours are 300 mm deep and we suggest that should be the minimum. Use simple butt joints to assemble the boxes, using wood glue and 30 mm jolt-head nails at close intervals to reinforce the corners. Cut out D-shaped hand-holes and nail the ends to the edge of the bottom before adding the sides.

47

TIMBER PLATE RACK

This timber plate rack looks like an antique but it's brand new! Approximately 600 mm wide, 1100 mm tall and 300 mm deep, each compartment is 100 mm wide and holds two bowls or up to eight plates. Use 35 x 19 mm timber for horizontal dividers, 12 mm dowel for vertical dividers and 300 x 19 mm maple planking for sides.

• Cut sides with a fretsaw to make a curved 200 x 40 mm indent on top front corners.

• Mark position of horizontals on sides: compartment heights are 250 mm (top), 300 mm (middle) and 350 mm (bottom); these can vary. Rear horizontals are 75 mm from back edge and bottom horizontals 75 mm from bottom edge (to avoid plate breakage). To cope with different sized plates, front horizontals are set at 120 mm, 140 mm, 160 mm, and 180 mm from the rear horizontals. At marked positions cut 35 x 19 x 10 mm-deep mortices into sides except for top horizontals.

• Cut out horizontals: allow extra 10 mm at either end to fit into mortices on all except top two. Mark all dowel intersection points on horizontals at same time to ensure accuracy.

• Drill 12 mm holes in rear horizontals. In the front drill 14 mm holes to allow the 12 mm dowel to continue through all horizontals, sloping outwards. Note that for top and bottom horizontals the drill should stop short to hold the dowel ends.

• Assemble all but the top two horizontals using white glue and 25 mm jolt-head nails. Push the 12 mm dowels down through their lines of holes.

• Lastly slot the top two horizontals in place, nailing through sides into simple butt joints. Punch nails, fill, stain and lacquer.

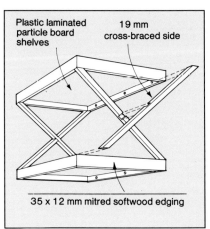

Plastic laminated particle board shelves

19 mm cross-braced side

35 x 12 mm mitred softwood edging

SERVING HATCH

Construct a butt-joint frame from laminated particle board incorporating a lower shelf for small storage jars. Divide it along the centre, make the top shelf open for two-way storage and ensure adequate head height for working below. Fix unit to masonry or locate wall studs, drilling holes for wall plugs.

CROSS-BRACED SHELVES

Criss-cross support struts add rigidity and load-bearing capacity to these elegant shelves, and the 35 mm-deep edges around four sides of each shelf add further strength. Make shelves from 300 mm-wide plastic-laminated particle board.

Mark out the number and spacing of the shelves on your wall before you start. Use mitred lengths of 35 x 12 mm softwood to edge the shelves, fixed with 35 mm countersunk screws and high-strength wood glue. The timber edges extend below the bottom surface of the shelf to enable you to fix the shelves to your wall at the back edge. Drill through the back edging piece first and then into the wall. Use 40 mm countersunk screws to fix the shelves in place at approximately 300 mm centres. Add the cross-braced supports made from 19 mm timber last; make the cross by sawing and chiselling a half-lap joint at the centre. Fit the ends of the braces at the horizontal angle of the shelves and drill and screw through each end into the timber shelving edges. The shelves hang from and bear down on the cross supports.

TRIPLE-TIERED TOWEL RACK

Cut shelves about 400 mm long from 300 x 25 mm pine, making each shelf about 25 mm deeper than the one above it. Cut shelf supports from 50 x 25 mm pine for the top shelf; 75 x 25 mm for the centre shelf; 100 x 25 mm for the lower shelf. Cut each pair of supports to the depth of the appropriate shelf.

Cut verticals from 50 x 25 mm pine and notch to take the supports. Curve the fronts of shelves and supports. Glue and nail supports in place, drill and fit 19 mm dowel in the lower supports. Nail the top shelf in place. Notch centre and lower shelves to fit around the verticals; glue and nail in place. Sand and apply clear matt finish. Screw metal angles to top and bottom shelf to fit to the wall.

BATHROOM HOLD-ALL

Build the cabinet with 19 mm-thick timber either flush with the wall or protruding from it.

Begin by making a simple box frame 435 mm high and 360 mm wide with 115 mm-wide timber. Butt join two or three 100 mm-deep shelves level with the cabinet back. Include 19 x 12 mm battens along the back to screw cabinet to wall.

Make the frame from an architrave moulding. Make the door frame of 42 x 19 mm timber. Sand the inner edge to a rounded finish and rout out a 20 x 10 mm recess on the same edge.

Cut the door frame to the dimensions shown, using a plain mitred frame or a half-butt joint (as illustrated). Have 4 mm mirror glass cut to fit it and tack a 3 mm plywood back into the back of the door to hold it in place. Use 35 mm hinges to hang the door. Fit a catch and handle.

Build the cabinet into the wall at this stage, continuing the wall lining behind the frame. Nail a 510 x 50 x 19 mm false sill to the bottom ends of the frame and trim beneath it with 19 mm quad. For the protruding version, allow both the sill and the trim to extend back to tiles or walls as shown in diagrams. A false sill gives a neat finish.

Diagram labels: 460 mm, 115 mm, Outer frame, Top, Door frame, 490 mm, 415 mm, 42 mm, Bottom sill, Sill trim, Tiles, 320 mm, 70 mm

EFFICIENT MEDICINE CABINET

Storing potions and prescriptions calls for a special type of shelving — it needs to be small in scale and shallow. By making this cabinet so that it opens halfway through its depth, its compartment-type shelves are not too deep and allow a clear view and easy access to contents.

For easy cleaning, all components were made from 13 mm plastic-laminated particle board. Cut components from the smallest pre-laminated shelves available as these already have laminated edges. Cut out all the components with the finished edges to the front of the shelves and the corresponding edges of the top, bottom and sides. Finish all other visible raw edges with iron-on laminate. To finish the outside surfaces of the doors and obscure the sawn edges of the sides, top and bottom, score and cut the entire surface from the sheet of plastic laminate and use contact adhesive to fix the sheets in place.

Cut out all the components indicated in the drawing and the Materials List and assemble the three boxes with wood glue and 30 mm panel pins. Although the photograph shows mitre joints it is easier to use butt joints — dimensions given are for butt joints. Carefully punch and fill the nail holes and retouch with enamel paint to match. Fit 50 mm butt hinges, spring door catches and drill through the doors to fit door handles.

Leave the cabinet doors plain as pictured, or use them as a source of decoration with an applied 'frame' of timber or plastic beading. Or they could be faced with mirror.

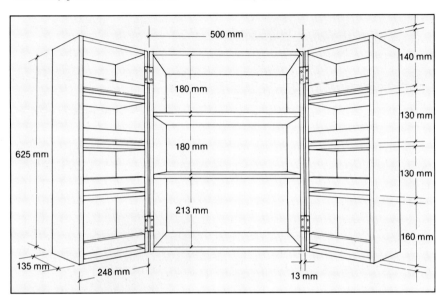

MATERIALS LIST

All components are cut from 13 mm plastic-laminated particleboard		
Item	**Size (in mm)**	**No.**
Cabinet sides	625 x 135	2
Cabinet top / bottom	474 x 135	1 each
Cabinet shelves	474 x 122	2
Cabinet back	599 x 474	1
Door sides	625 x 135	4
Door top / bottom	222 x 135	2 each
Door fronts	599 x 222	2
Door shelves	222 x 122	6
Door shelf fronts	222 x 30	8

Other. Iron-on plastic laminate strip edging: 1 sheet or off-cuts plastic laminate; wood glue; 30 mm panel pins; four 50 mm butt hinges; 2 spring door catches; door handles.

BATHSIDE TROLLEY

Successful projects are essentially practical as well as beautiful and this trolley will be a pleasure to make and a delight to use. Though modern in concept, it fits quite easily into a traditional or period bathroom. The curved bathside trolley is mounted on castors making it possible to position it with fingertip control from the comfort of the bath. Use it for oils and lotions, reading matter, a cup of tea or even a glass of wine. Lie back, relax and enjoy your bath in truly Sybaritic style.

• Mark out two semicircular shapes on 16 mm plastic-laminated particle board. They should have a 230 mm radius and an additional 230 mm depth at the straight edges.

• Cut out the curved shapes with a jigsaw and cover the exposed end grain edges with iron-on edging tape.

• Cut three 35 mm dowels to match the height of the bath, taking into account the height of the castors and the two semicircular shelves.

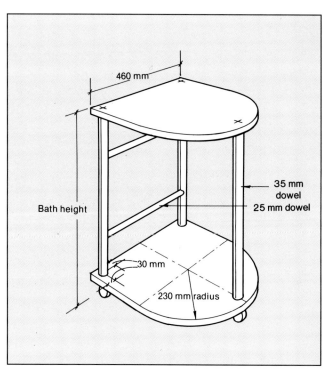

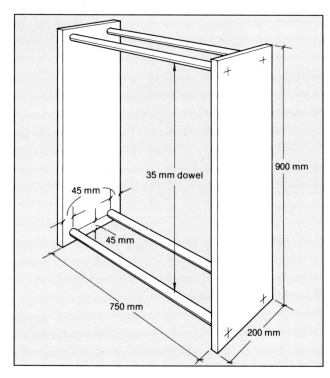

• Drill and insert two 400 mm lengths of 25 mm dowel horizontally between two of the 35 mm dowels to make the back leg structure.

• Drill and insert 45 mm particle board screws through the two particle board shelves into the ends of the three dowels. To conceal their heads in the top shelf of the trolley, use white sleeves and screw caps. After you have driven the screw home, fit the conical sleeve over the screw when inserting and clipping the cap in place. Lastly, screw castors in place.

TOWEL RACK

This freestanding rack is an update of the old style, elegantly turned model. The simplified design makes it very easy to build.

• Cut two 900 x 200 mm rectangles from 16 mm plastic-laminated particle board. Some timber yards will finish the edges for you. Otherwise apply iron-on edging tape.

• Cut four 750 mm lengths of 35 mm dowel. Drill, glue and screw them in place as indicated in the diagram, using screw caps to conceal the screw heads.

BATHROOM SHELVING

If shelving does not extend to the walls at one or both ends, sides will be needed to complete the shelving 'box' before the whole unit is fastened in place. Design the unit to line up with other fixtures on the bathroom wall such as a large mirror over the basin.

Make the shelves from 200 mm-wide timber planking with simple butt joints. Fix a 40 x 18 mm support batten to the wall to coincide with the under-surface of the top shelf and fix unit to it. Add extra support with 35 mm angle brackets.

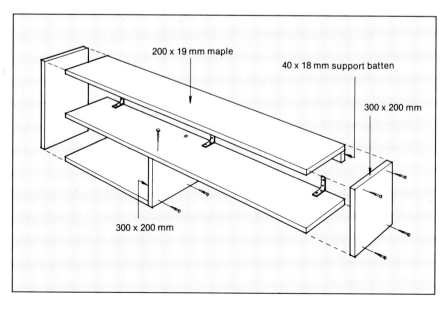

200 x 19 mm maple

40 x 18 mm support batten

300 x 200 mm

300 x 200 mm

THE HOME OFFICE

COPING WITH THE HOUSEHOLD PAPERWORK

The paperwork of modern life is expanding at an alarming rate. In the early stages of every household, bills, receipts and documents can be kept in one manila folder. The next step is a concertina file and when that starts to disintegrate, a decision has to be made about a more solid and permanent system. Box files, one for each subject, kept on shelves are a possibility. On the other hand, a filing cabinet seems like a sensible plan for storing appliance guarantees and instructions, health and immunisation records for two- and four-legged members of the family, school reports, birth certificates, etc., etc. . . . but where can it be located? The home computer has also become a vital part of modern domestic life and it needs a place (preferably away from the casual and frequently noisy atmosphere of the family room) where it can be safely positioned and used in peace.

A separate study would be the ideal but there are relatively few people who can afford to put a whole room aside for the purposes of home records, or even business or study. A nook in a hall or a corridor could be just the place.

If the only possibility is to incorporate a work centre unobtrusively into a living or family room, try to isolate it from sound and activity. Cover the top and sides of such a space with acoustic tiles for a degree of quiet and bring in a portable folding screen to deflect traffic and keep the milling hordes away.

Good lighting, a comfortable chair and the phone are essentials. A successful work space will also have a desk or benchtop with shelving that not only looks as if it belongs in the room but complements and enhances the overall layout.

A hide-away study centre which is concealed by louvre doors when not in use (see page 58)

COMPACT HOUSEHOLD BUSINESS CENTRE

If space is limited, you have to think and plan on the small side. This narrow benchtop and recessed shelving serves as the household business centre without taking up too much space. In designing a compact centre like this one, make use of any irregularities in the shape of the room. This unit is built in an awkward spot between a protruding window and one of the room's internal corners.

Careful selection of materials gives the unit a high-quality finish. The large brackets which support the desk are made from 50 mm brushbox, and may be dowel-joined to the bottom of the particle board carcass or screwed from inside. For the rest, choose a particle board with a veneer which is similar in colour. Drawers are ready-made 450 x 400 mm units, with veneered particle board fronts.

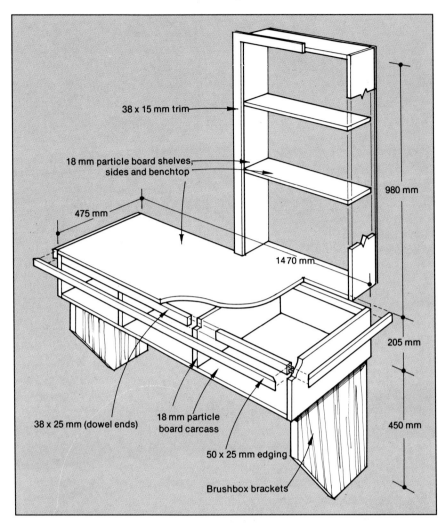

38 x 15 mm trim

18 mm particle board shelves, sides and benchtop

980 mm

475 mm

1470 mm

205 mm

38 x 25 mm (dowel ends)

18 mm particle board carcass

50 x 25 mm edging

450 mm

Brushbox brackets

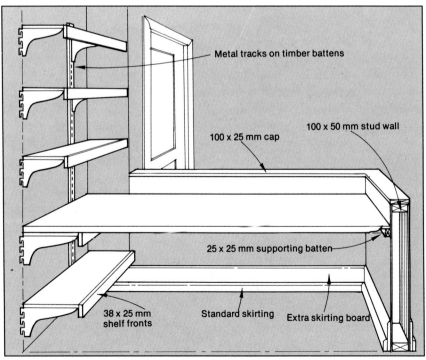

Metal tracks on timber battens

100 x 25 mm cap

100 x 50 mm stud wall

25 x 25 mm supporting batten

38 x 25 mm shelf fronts

Standard skirting

Extra skirting board

A CORNER OFFICE

By using materials which match the style of the room, even an 'office' as big as this one will blend unobtrusively into an unused corner.

The low divider, with lower benchtop, is finished in white plastic laminate and pine, merging perfectly with detailing in the room. Skirting boards continue around the divider, with a deeper board above for a tailored look. The plastic-laminated shelving has an edging of pine, and metal shelving tracks are mounted on timber battens.

Purchased drawer unit on castors beneath the bench provides mobile, hidden storage for small items.

WORKING FROM HOME

The ultimate in decentralisation is working from home. The work station principle, devised and spawned by high rental, high-rise office buildings, can move into the home with ease — and be upgraded at the same time. Essentials are comfort and efficiency. Have a good office chair and install good general and specific-task lighting. There is a trend away from fluorescent tubes to tungsten lights because they are easier on the eyes and more aesthetically pleasing. At home, hopefully, natural light can form a major part of the illumination. You need not be bound by the rather bleak lines of office furniture. As long as there is the required amount of space for a computer, fax and 'phone, have a lovingly home made work surface and storage unit.

HIDE-AWAY STUDY CENTRE

This study centre can be built into an alcove or large cupboard as long as it is a minimum of 400 mm deep. The success of this design depends to a large extent on the flush fit of the louvre doors when closed. When planning and measuring, remember to leave sufficient space for this at the front of the unit.

Look at the diagram for a basic construction guide. Decide what your requirements are for the study centre and draw a plan on graph paper. The total height of the unit will be about 1800–2000 mm (try to make it the same as doors in the rest of the house), and a comfortable desk height is about 750 mm. Divide up shelving space to suit your needs, remembering that shelves have to be recessed by about 40 mm to allow the desk to fold up. The drop-down benchtop gives you extra working space; above and below it plan large and small pigeonholes to provide super-efficient storage. Deep drawers below give further filing space.

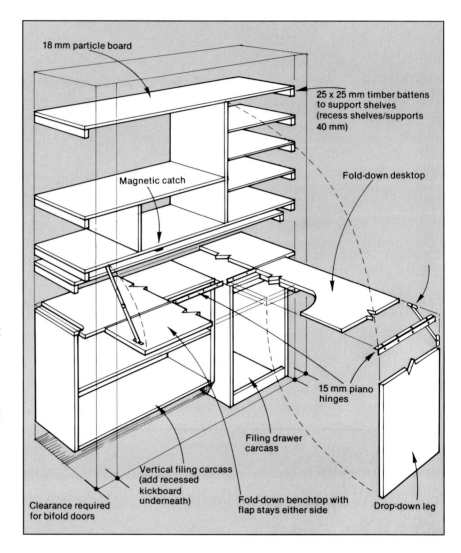

18 mm particle board

25 x 25 mm timber battens to support shelves (recess shelves/supports 40 mm)

Magnetic catch

Fold-down desktop

15 mm piano hinges

Filing drawer carcass

Vertical filing carcass (add recessed kickboard underneath)

Fold-down benchtop with flap stays either side

Drop-down leg

Clearance required for bifold doors

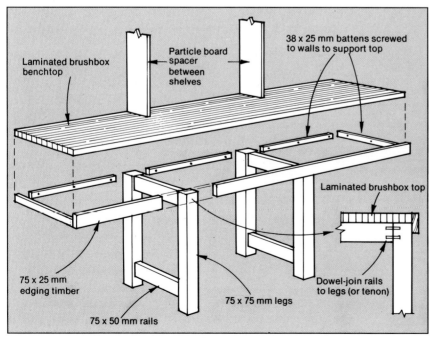

Laminated brushbox benchtop

Particle board spacer between shelves

38 x 25 mm battens screwed to walls to support top

Laminated brushbox top

75 x 25 mm edging timber

Dowel-join rails to legs (or tenon)

75 x 75 mm legs

75 x 50 mm rails

FLOOR-TO-CEILING STORAGE

Sometimes the least complicated solution may be to turn one whole wall over to a new built-in. This will give it a bold simplicity which will also prevent the room becoming too fragmented. This floor-to-ceiling study centre actually helped the shape of the room in the picture by cutting down on its length.

The basis of the unit is easy-to-assemble industrial metal shelving, which is available in a wide range of sizes. The desk is a slab of laminated brushbox mounted on a framework supported by four 75 x 75 mm posts. The space underneath can house small filing cabinets.

FURNITURE AND DOORS

STYLISH DECORATIVE FEATURES FOR THE HOME

It is in decorating and furnishing that the greatest challenges (and the most fun) await the workshop enthusiast. Timber can be cut, smoothed and finished to give the warmth and essence of craftsmanship which is so often lacking in today's mass-produced furniture. And there is no need to 'make do' with a shelving unit which is a little too large or small for the available space or a table which will not comfortably accommodate a certain number of chairs. Custom furnishing provides opportunities for fine quality and solidity in a world where cheap, light and short-lasting have become the norm.

Modern glues, fixings and finishes have made the pieces illustrated in this chapter tougher and more stable than furniture from past eras. Power tools hurry up the home manufacturing process and compensate more than adequately for the shortage of time in the modern world. But the fact that an addition to the stock of household furniture is quicker and easier to make than in the past does not detract from its worth or from the plaudits accorded its creator. Electric sanders and planes can even enhance individuality by giving the more accomplished handyperson the opportunity to add a personal style to standard designs. And it is the conjunction of these finishing touches, the slight changes in levels and the shadows of grooves which impart the designer signature to furniture produced in the home workshop and make it worthy of star billing in every room.

A decorative shelf unit for displaying your household treasures (see page 62)

DECORATIVE SHELF UNIT

An attractive wall-hung cabinet can be used to display a collection of china or simply store everyday items. Made of pine, the unit has been painted and then 'aged'.

1. Tools required: circular saw, jigsaw, electric drill, cordless screwdriver, orbital sander, square, tape measure, hammers, plane.

2. Copy the shape of the side (see page 64) onto a piece of paper and transfer the outline onto each of the two side pieces.

3. Cut along the marked lines with a jigsaw.

4. Similarly cut out the scalloped valance.

5. Cut the three shelves, the top and the base to length, ensuring that the ends are exactly square.

6. With a jigsaw, cut out a section at the back of the top and base to accommodate the tongue-and-groove boards.

7. Mark the positions of the shelves on the inside of each side. Predrill and countersink the screw holes.

8. Drill corresponding holes in the ends of the shelves. This will assist with the location of the shelves during assembly.

9. Using 40 mm countersunk screws, attach the shelves to the sides. (Note. 50 mm nails may be used instead of screws.)

10. Attach valance with 30 mm nails.

11. Screw top and base to sides.

12. Use a plane and then sandpaper to round the top edges and ends of the plate stops. Nail them to the

shelves with 25 mm brads. Their position is determined by the depth of the plate or bowl to be supported. (This step may be omitted if the shelf will not be used to hold plates.)

13. Fill screw holes with wood filler.

14. Cut the tongue-and-groove boards to length, ensuring that the ends are square, and nail them in place with 30 mm nails. The outside boards should have their tongue or groove planed off to give a smooth finish. It is important to ensure that the unit is exactly square and the ends of the boards line up neatly.

15. Cut the quad to length and mitre the front corners. Nail it under the top with 30 mm nails.

16. Sand the filled screw and nail holes until smooth.

17. Round the front edges of the shelves and sides with a hand plane or sandpaper to give them a well-worn feel. Drill and countersink four holes in suitable positions on the back of the unit to fix it to the wall.

18. Paint the unit with blue acrylic paint.

19. When the paint is dry, wrap a tinful of old nuts, bolts, screws and nails in a strong rag and hit all exposed surface and edges with the bundle to give it an aged look.

20. Rub the unit down with sandpaper and steel wool (do not use soap pads). On all parts which should show wear, such as the shelf edges and the back boards where the plates rest, rub the paint off to expose the wood beneath. Apply two or three coats of clear matt polyurethane, sanding lightly between coats. When dry, screw to wall with countersunk screws long enough to grip the wall securely.

1

5

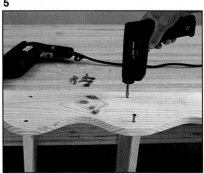

9

13

17

MATERIALS LIST

Item	Material (in mm)	Length (in mm)	No.
Side	170 x 19 pine	1162	2
Shelf	170 x 19 pine	890	3
Top and base	212 x 19 pine	1000	2
Valance	80 x 12 pine	928	1
Back	140 x 12 T & G pine	1200	7
Moulding	19 x 19 pine quad	1500	1
Plate stop	19 x 12 pine	830	4

Other. 40 mm countersunk screws; 30 mm bullet-head nails; 25 mm brads; wood filler; blue acrylic paint; clear matt polyurethane.

2

3

4

6

7

8

10

11

12

14

15

16

18

19

20

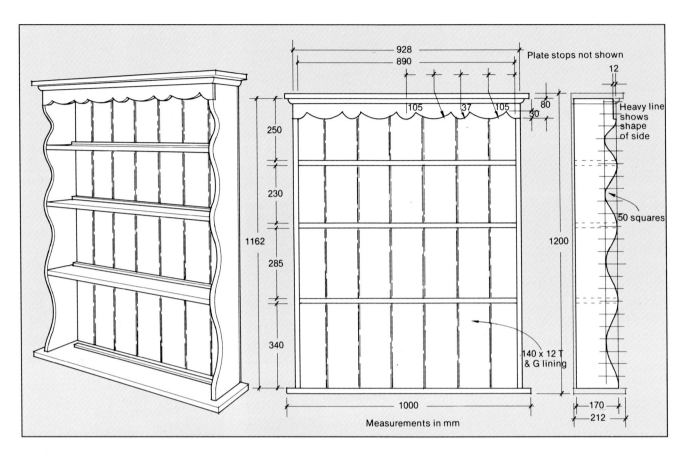

928
890
Plate stops not shown
12
105 37 105
80
30
250
Heavy line shows shape of side
230
50 squares
1162
1200
285
140 x 12 T & G lining
340
1000
170
212
Measurements in mm

WINDOW SEAT

From a storage point of view, simple lift-up lid box seating can be an asset just about anywhere in the home. Decide on the best position, and build the box to fit the space. The window seat pictured is 550 mm deep (half the depth of the alcove), 450 mm high (allowing the 100 mm-thick foam to sit beneath the windowsill) and the full 1600 mm length of the bay window. There are three main stages to construction.

The first is the box itself. Use 18 mm thick particle board for the purpose and include four sides, the back one being a simple way to support the top without constructing a fully load-bearing frame.

Next, make the frame which fits around the top edge of the box. The frame is basically an E-shaped piece which fits over the rear, ends and centre of the box. Use 19 mm softwood, 70 mm wide for the main frame. The centre of the frame and two end supports fix to the underside of the main frame to provide ledges on which the lids will rest, and these are made from 42 mm-wide timber.

Lastly, cut the pair of lids to size and hinge them in place. Two lids were used in the window box illustrated for easy lifting. Another method is to have the lid as one large piece. Finish with the fascia board across the front. Cushion the seat with 100 mm-thick medium-density foam covered with material to match the furnishings.

Step-by-step
1. Begin by constructing the basic four-sided particle board box. Glue and nail the vertical butt joints in four places at each corner.

2. Make sure the box fills the entire alcove, removing wall cladding and skirting boards where necessary to get

1

3

5

a flush fit. Nail the box to timber wall studs.

3. Start making the frame by cutting 70 x 19 mm timber the full length of the box for the rear piece. Screw the 42 x 19 mm central support to the underside of this piece, leaving a gap of 18 mm at the end.

4. For the end frames, screw the end supports to the frame ends, allowing them to extend 18 mm along one side, plus 52 mm at one end (this joins to the underside of the rear frame piece to form the corner joint). Note too to allow the frame ends to extend 18 mm at the opposite end — this will rest on the particle board box at front.

5. Assemble the framework, place on box and nail and glue the ends in place, making sure that the centre and end supports finish flush with the top edge of the particle board.

6. Support the centre piece at the front

2

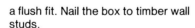

4

6

7

on a short bearing plate, rebated and screwed to the inside of the particle board. Hold the fascia timber in place while fixing to prevent particle board bending.

7. Hinge the lids in place and drill 20 mm finger pull holes in the centre front of each. Include a 70 mm-deep fascia across the front. It should sit 15 mm above the particle board edge to hold the cushioning in place.

STORAGE PLUS TABLE FOR TWO

This slender unit will fit into a sliver of space protruding only 30 cm when collapsed and is a mere 90 cm deep with its gateleg and top in position ready for snacks or doing the household accounts. China and glassware can be stored attractively in a wallhung storage unit. At mealtimes, this handsome built-in can be transformed into table space for two. Construction is almost as simple as its one-step folding action. Study the diagrams and pictures to see how the gateleg folds out to support the tabletop.

Cut out all the components listed. Use a jigsaw to cut the curves on shelf sides, gateleg and tabletop to the radii shown on the diagrams. Drill, glue and screw all joints throughout assembly.

Shelf unit. Start by fastening the cleat to the underside back edge of the top shelf. Saw 19 mm off the depth of the bottom shelf. Assemble shelves and sides. Complete with

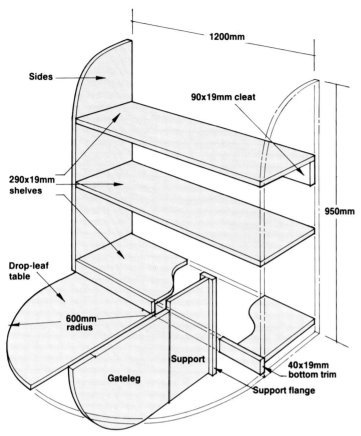

Sides

90x19mm cleat

1200mm

950mm

290x19mm shelves

Drop-leaf table

600mm radius

Support

Gateleg

40x19mm bottom trim

Support flange

MATERIALS LIST		
Item	Material	Length (in mm)
Sides	290 x 19 mm pine	950
Shelves	290 x 19 mm pine	1200
Cleat	90 x 19 mm pine	1200
Bottom trim	40 x 19 mm pine	1200
Support flange	70 x 19 mm pine	450
Support	240 x 19 mm pine	450
Gateleg	18 mm high-density particle board	450 x 410
Dropleaf	18 mm high-density particle board	1200 x 600

Other. 400 mm piano hinging; 1100 mm piano hinging; 35 mm countersunk screws; piano hinge screws; glue; paint.

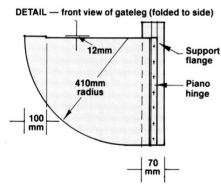

DETAIL — front view of gateleg (folded to side)

12mm

Support flange

410mm radius

Piano hinge

100 mm

70 mm

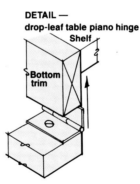

DETAIL — drop-leaf table piano hinge

Shelf

Bottom trim

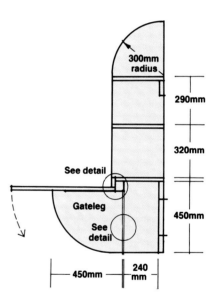

300mm radius

290mm

320mm

450mm

See detail

Gateleg

See detail

450mm

240 mm

the bottom trim, flush with the bottom of the sides.

Gateleg. Screw through the back of the support flange into the back edge of the particle board support, using four screws, evenly spaced. To allow the gateleg to swing freely, saw 12 mm off its top edge for all but the front 100 mm. Using the 400 mm length of piano hinging, screw the gateleg to the front edge of the support (see detail diagram). Drill through the support flange

and screw the whole support structure to wall, with the top at table height.

To finish. Sit the shelving unit on the top of the gateleg and screw through the cleat to wall-mount the unit. Screw through the bottom shelf into the top of the support. Use the 1100 mm length of piano hinging to fix the dropleaf to the front trim (see detail diagram). Finish with paint.

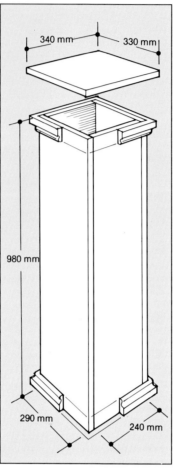

340 mm / 330 mm

980 mm

290 mm / 240 mm

PEDESTAL

Frequently a furniture layout can leave a corner without any practical purpose. With a pedestal, a plant or prized object can be elevated to give a corner importance.

Make the pairs of sides from 290 x 19 mm and 240 x 19 mm pine planks. By using simple butt joints, the finished size will be 290 x 280 mm. Make the top 340 x 330 mm, with a join across the centre. Use mitred colonial skirting to trim the top and bottom.

RUSTIC TIMBER DOOR

Screw rough-sawn timber planks to a sheet of 18 mm exterior grade plywood cut to fit the door opening. Countersink screws and glue wood plugs over the heads. Hang with strap hinges and install latch hardware.

Use this method of applying a decorative cladding of any style to a basic plain plywood base cut to fit the door opening. Smooth planks with bevelled edges could be laid vertically, horizontally or diagonally on the base door. Cut the planks level with the perimeter of the door or make allowance for a mitred frame which could be picked out in a contrasting colour of paint or stain.

FAMILY SIZED PINE TABLE

This generous table, built in pine using readily available timber in standard sizes, has the great appeal of being straightforward to make. And like so many simple things, it is also very attractive. Cut cross pieces, leg and top pieces to lengths given in the materials list. Leave the side and end trim pieces until the rest of the table is completed.

Dowel, glue and clamp the legs to the lower cross pieces using two 50mm-long dowels per joint. Screw the tops of the legs to the upper cross pieces as shown in the diagram, using two 50 mm screws per joint. Screw the centre cross piece to the leg braces, and the side support blocks to the ends of the cross piece using 50 mm screws. Screw the top pieces, with 5 mm gaps between, to the upper and centre cross pieces with 30 mm screws from underneath.

Measure the actual size of the top, mitre side and end trim pieces to fit and screw them to the upper cross pieces and side support blocks from the inside with 50 mm screws. Secure the corners with two 30 mm panel pins per joint. Fill holes and gaps, sand and finish with two coats of clear polyurethane.

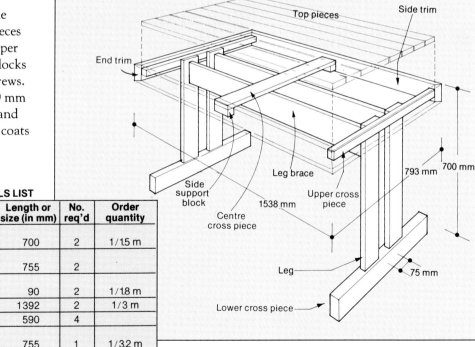

MATERIALS LIST

Item	Materials	Length or size (in mm)	No. req'd	Order quantity
Lower cross piece	90 x 35 mm pine	700	2	1 / 1.5 m
Upper cross piece	35 x 35 mm pine	755	2	
Side support blocks	35 x 35 mm pine	90	2	1 / 1.8 m
Leg braces	140 x 19 mm pine	1392	2	1 / 3 m
Legs	90 x 19 mm pine	590	4	
Centre cross piece	90 x 19 mm pine	755	1	1 / 3.2 m
Top	90 x 19 mm pine	1500	8	8 / 1.5 m
End trim	90 x 19 mm pine	793	2	
Side trim	90 x 19 mm pine	1538	2	2 / 2.4 m

Other. 400 mm x 10 mm dia. dowel; 30 mm x 10 g countersunk wood screws; 50 mm x 10 g countersunk wood screws; 60 mm x 10 g countersunk wood screws; 30 mm panel pins; white glue; polyurethane.

STEP-UP LIBRARY TROLLEY

With steps which fold away and shelves in the one mobile unit, this sturdy addition to the home library provides storage for everyday volumes and items, and gives access to high shelves as well. The steps fold neatly against the side of the roll-around shelving unit — they're less cumbersome than a similar purchased set.

Begin by making the shelving. Cut the five lengths of timber (see materials list) and glue and screw the three shelves between the two sides, positioning the top and bottom shelves 50 mm from the ends of the sides.

Round off the top outside corners of the two 700 mm-long verticals and attach them to the shelving sides, screwing from the inside. Cut out all the step-framing components and round their ends.

Start assembling the structure from the bottom, following diagram. Pay special attention to all the pivoting points. The 25 mm-long screws can be in a variety of gauges up to 7 mm thick. Remember, when drilling the pivoting screw joints, the screws should move freely through the first piece of timber and grip firmly into the second. Drill all the pivoting screw joints from the outside.

Fix the foldaway steps to the outer edge of each vertical, allowing enough room for the structure to move and fold up. Screw the steps in place. Finish the whole piece with polyurethane and use contact adhesive to glue the rubber sheeting to shelves and steps. Drill and insert castors in place with mounting blocks if necessary to lift the unit.

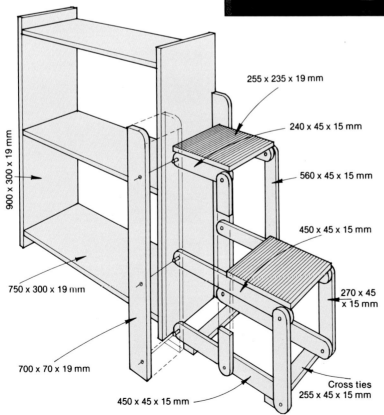

255 x 235 x 19 mm

240 x 45 x 15 mm

560 x 45 x 15 mm

450 x 45 x 15 mm

270 x 45 x 15 mm

900 x 300 x 19 mm

750 x 300 x 19 mm

700 x 70 x 19 mm

450 x 45 x 15 mm

Cross ties
255 x 45 x 15 mm

MATERIALS LIST

Item	Material	Size or length (in mm)	No.
Sides	300 x 19 mm pine	900	2
Shelves	300 x 19 mm pine	750	3
Verticals	70 x 19 mm pine	700	2
	45 x 15 mm pine	560	2
	45 x 15 mm pine	270	2
Horizontals	45 x 15 mm pine	450	4
	45 x 15 mm pine	240	2
Cross ties	45 x 15 mm pine	255	2
Steps	19 mm ply	255 x 235	2

Other. One square metre of ribbed grip rubber; wood glue; 35 mm countersunk screws; 25 mm countersunk screws; four castors; polyurethane; contact adhesive for rubber.

RESTORING A DOOR

Many a dim room will live to sparkle another day with the additional light that shines through bright new glass panels. They're great for ill-lit hallways, but also an excellent little lighting trick to play anywhere in the house. If privacy is a problem, use frosted opaque glass instead of transparent panes, or choose glass with an attractive Victorian pattern.

1. Carefully lever beading off so timber is not damaged.
2. Pull out nails with pincers.

3. Drill a hole at each inner corner of the beading line. Use a jigsaw to remove the rectangle formed by the holes. (The beading on the other side of the door remains.)
4. Clean the rebate.
5. Apply putty to the rebate.
6. Press in precut glass panel, with smooth side facing you if glass is rippled or etched.
7. Secure glass with pins.
8. Apply a little putty to the beading you have removed.
9. Secure with skew nails, punch in, fill and sand. Finish door as desired.

1

2

3

4

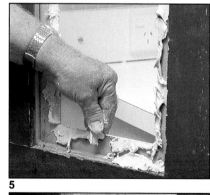

5

6

7

8

9

GIFTS

A gift which emerges from the home workshop is a symbol of devotion and is as far removed as possible from the commercialisation of festivals such as Christmas. Although the outlay for homemade gifts is small (the scrap pile of offcuts can frequently supply sufficient materials for all manner of projects), the time and effort invested may be considerable, so preplanning is essential. The workshop cannot produce last-minute stocking fillers.

If the workbench is to be the scene of creation for a batch of homemade gifts, it may be advisable to rationalise the steps and procedures and do a little assembly-line production. Cut out all the same or similar sections at one time, then do the gluing, screwing and fixing at the next session and later the finishing but leaving plenty of time for paints, varnishes and polyurethanes to dry completely.

Apply all finishes at the one time after the workshop has been thoroughly cleaned and vacuumed and any remaining dust and particles allowed to settle. Remember that most finishes will give timber a yellowy glow. If a more bleached, white look is desired, 'lime' the timber with thinned plastic or oil paint. Brush it on and then rub off the excess with a rag before the white obscures the grain completely. Allow the paint to dry thoroughly before applying a compatible sealing finish.

It is on small items that stencils and painted decoration are particularly appropriate. And a completely original design or an individual combination of several standard decorative elements such as squiggles, leaves and lines can give homemade gifts great distinction.

Pay special attention to the fit and finish of a gift — it will be under scrutiny and admired from all possible angles and the creator won't be able to arrange for its 'best' side to be presented for public view.

Hand-crafted workboxes make welcome gifts (see page 74)

WORKBOXES

These two projects will be enjoyable homework for those who can't resist small and interesting designs for household accessories.

The larger of these two workboxes, designed as a knitting box, has a removable tray which fits above the main storage space. The small one, a sewing box, has a hinged lid on each side of the central handle. Either box may be adapted for other uses, such as the storage of toys or tools. Divisions can be added inside to organise the storage space if the box is to hold small items.

MATERIALS

Allowing for wastage and errors, the small box will use about 80 cm square of 9 mm plywood and the large box 1.2 square metres. Other. 25 mm nails, wood glue, fine sandpaper, wood stain (optional), paint markers, clear polyurethane. The small box will need four face-mounted hinges with short screws. The large box will need 415 mm of 19 mm-diameter dowel with two 25 mm screws for the handle.

1. Marking out. Copy the outlines of the parts from the diagram on to the plywood. The curved shapes may be drawn on paper, then transferred to the plywood with carbon paper.
2. Cutting out. Use a jigsaw to cut out the parts. The straight cuts are made simpler by clamping a straight piece of wood to the plywood to act as a guide for the jigsaw. The jigsaw blade must be sharp or it will tend to drift off the line. Note that for some cuts the jigsaw has to be set to an angle so that the cut edge will fit properly — these have been shown in the diagrams as bold lines.
3. Cutting curved shapes. When using the jigsaw to cut along the curved lines, some of the tight curves should be cut with a narrow blade to reduce the possibility of the blade jamming.
4. Assembly. Assemble the parts with 25 mm nails and wood glue. Drilling short pilot holes for the nails will make the assembly easier, as will an extra pair of hands to hold the parts together while you work. Apply the glue sparingly and clean up any excess with a moist rag. Punch the nail heads and fill the holes for a neater finish.
5. Sanding. Smooth all edges with sandpaper. If you intend to stain

1

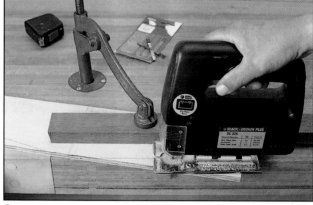

2

3

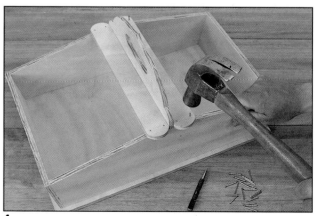

4

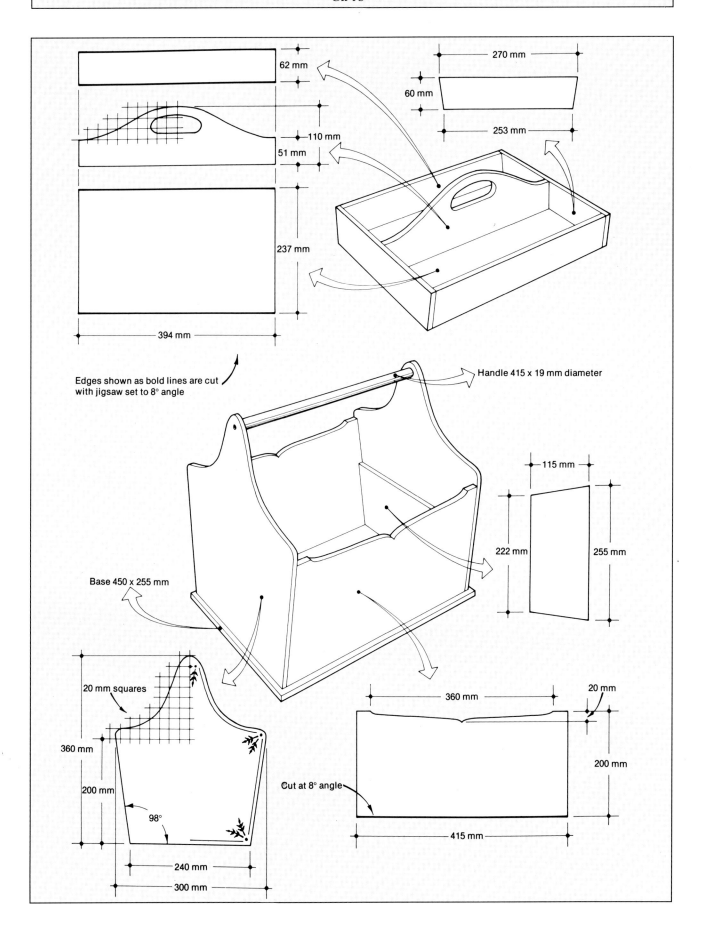

62 mm

270 mm

60 mm

253 mm

110 mm

51 mm

237 mm

394 mm

Edges shown as bold lines are cut
with jigsaw set to 8° angle

Handle 415 x 19 mm diameter

115 mm

222 mm

255 mm

Base 450 x 255 mm

20 mm squares

20 mm

360 mm

360 mm

200 mm

200 mm

98°

Cut at 8° angle

240 mm

415 mm

300 mm

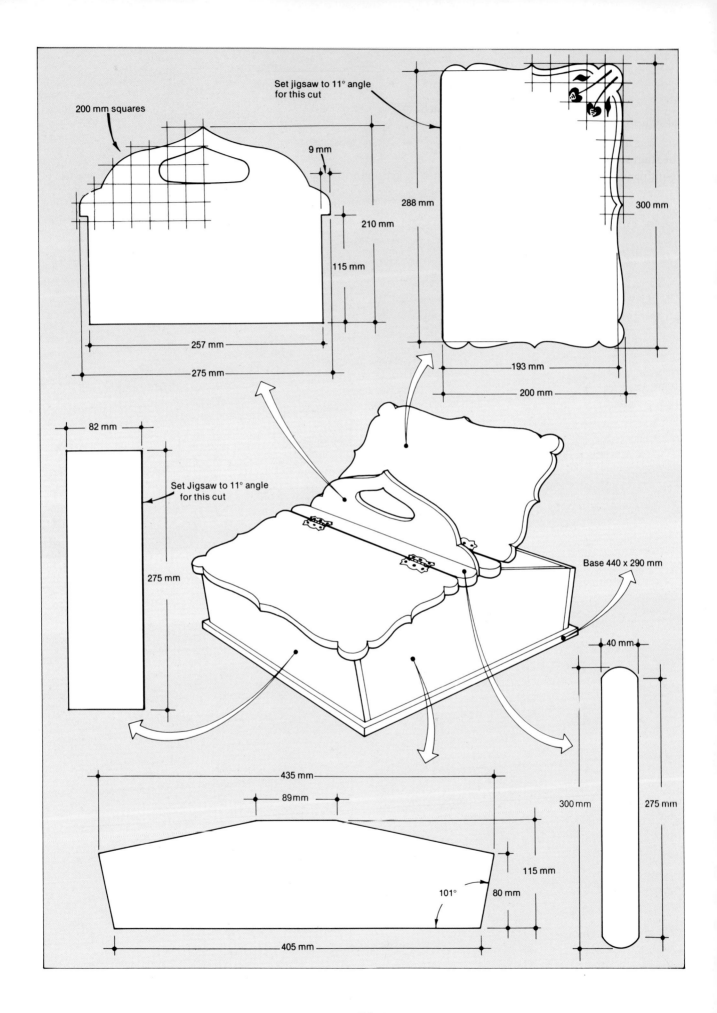

200 mm squares

Set jigsaw to 11° angle for this cut

9 mm

288 mm

210 mm

115 mm

300 mm

257 mm

275 mm

193 mm

200 mm

82 mm

Set Jigsaw to 11° angle for this cut

275 mm

Base 440 x 290 mm

40 mm

435 mm

89 mm

300 mm

275 mm

115 mm

101°

80 mm

405 mm

the box, make sure that all traces of glue are sanded off. Any remaining glue acts as a sealer which prevents the stain soaking into the wood, resulting in a patchy appearance.

6. Fixing handle of larger box. Fix the dowel handle to the ends with 25 mm countersunk screws. Drilling pilot holes will help.

7. Fixing hinges of smaller box.

Attach the facemounted brass hinges after marking out and drilling pilot holes for the screws.

8. Finishing. The boxes may be stained or left raw and then finished with clear polyurethane. After the boxes are sealed with the first coat of polyurethane, decorations of your own design may be applied with paint markers or stencils.

When they are dry, apply two more coats of polyurethane, sanding lightly between coats.

9. The smaller box was stained with a teak wood stain and decorated with a contrasting white floral design.

10. The larger box was left unstained and decorated with a black leaf design.

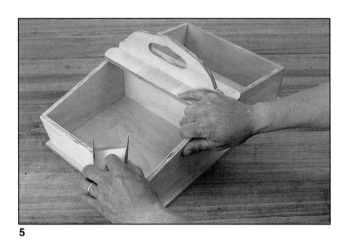

5

6

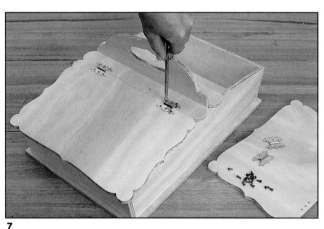

7

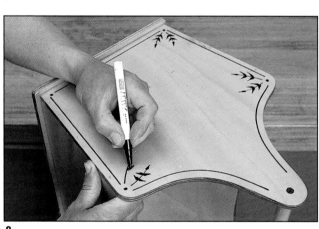

8

9

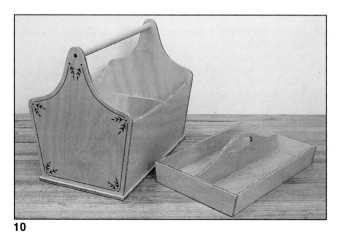

10

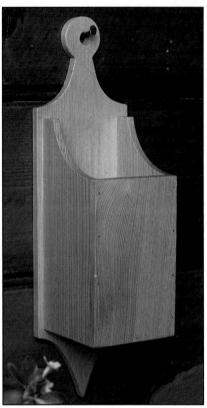

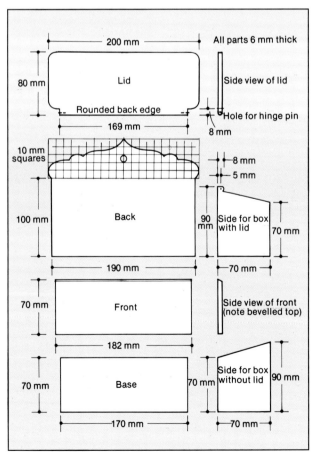

Boxes are equally attractive on the bench or hung on the wall.

A wall-hung utensil box keeps spoons handy; it looks lovely with trailing ivy (stand a small vase in the box), fresh or dried flowers.

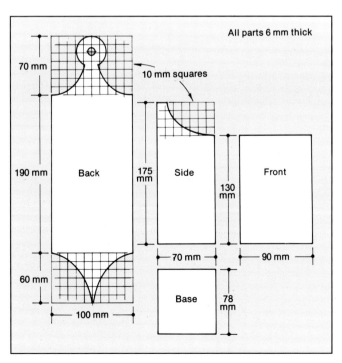

KITCHEN BOXES

The boxes may be made from 6 mm plywood, fine particle board (5 mm Craftwood) or solid timber. If solid wood is used, obtain some select grade pine or Western Red Cedar. Ask at a joinery to have the board planed down to a thickness of 7 or 8 mm. Be sure to cut out the pieces with the wood grain running in the direction which gives the most strength.

The measurements shown on the plans apply to 6 mm-thick material. If any other thickness is used, some allowances will have to be made. (The difference between the widths of the front and the base is twice the material thickness.)

CONSTRUCTION

Cut out the parts accurately and smooth the straight edges by rubbing them along 150 grit sandpaper held on a flat surface. Make the shaped pieces by marking the outline onto paper ruled in 10 mm squares and transferring the shape onto the wood using carbon paper. Cut out shapes by using a fretsaw, bandsaw or other suitable saw and carefully sand the edges.

Assemble the front, sides, base and back using small nails (20 x 1.25 mm) and PVA glue. Assembly will be assisted by pre-drilling all nail holes (to locate the parts) and holding the joints together with packaging tape until the glue is dry.

Make the hinge pins for the lidded box by cutting the heads off 2 mm-diameter nails. The pins should fit loosely in the sides of the box and tightly in the lid. Drill the pin holes with the lid placed in the closed position on the box.

FINISH

Natural timber boxes may be finished with a drying oil such as Cabot's Danish Oil or boiled linseed oil. For a more durable finish a clear satin polyurethane may be used. The particle board boxes may be painted and then decorated with stencils.

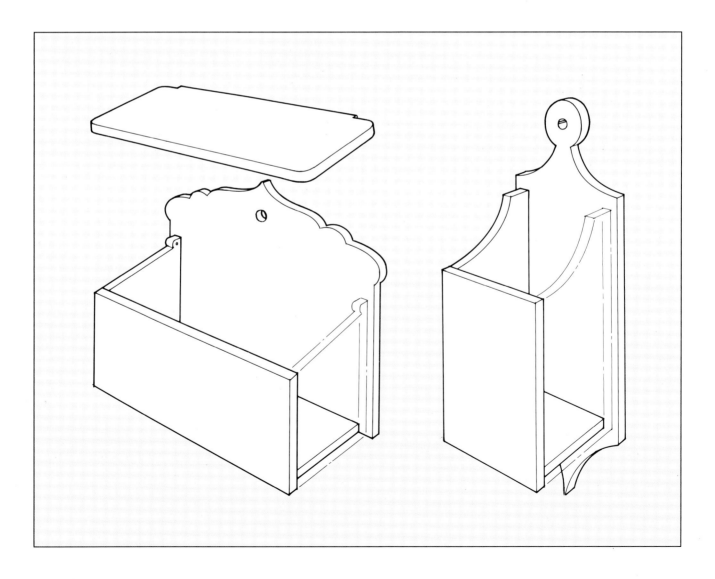

79

TRAY

The tray can be painted with bright gloss paint and decorated either freehand or with stencils and sealed with polyurethane.

1. Cut all pieces to the sizes given in the materials list and plane the edges straight.

2. Copy the outline of the end of the tray onto a piece of paper and transfer the shape onto the end pieces (by cutting out the shape or using carbon paper.)

3. Cut along the marked lines with a jigsaw. To cut out the internal shape of the handle, drill a hole to allow access for the jigsaw blade. Sand the cut edges to a smooth finish. (These shapes may be cut more accurately by using a router and a suitable template.)

4. Round corners of tray base.

5. Using a 5 mm 'rounding over' router bit, smooth outside edges of sides and ends. Similarly round over edges of tray base.

6. Mark out the positions of the sides and ends on the tray base and mark the screw positions. Pre-drill and countersink the screw holes.

7. Drill corresponding holes in the sides and ends (test on a scrap piece of Craftwood to select the most suitable hole size for the screws). The pre-drilling will assist with the location of the components and prevent them from splitting.

8. All components should now be ready for assembly. Apply a little PVA glue to each joint, assemble the sides and ends, then screw them to the base.

9. Fill the screw holes with wood filler. Sand all surfaces smooth with fine sandpaper and seal the tray with particle board sealer. Lightly sand when dry.

10. Apply two coats of gloss paint. If desired, decorate with stencilled designs or paint markers.

Once the painted design is dry, apply clear polyurethane finish.

1

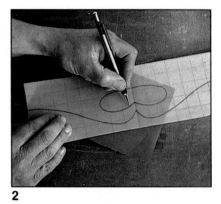

2

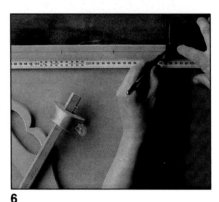

6

7

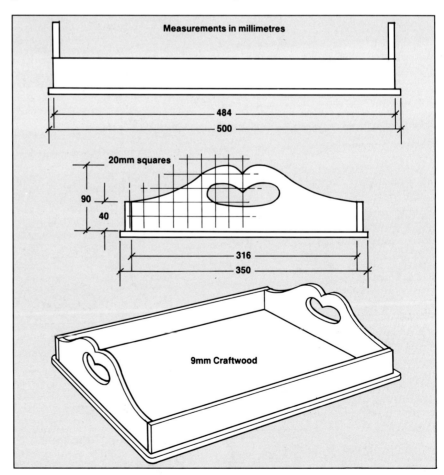

Measurements in millimetres

484
500

20mm squares

90
40

316
350

9mm Craftwood

3

4

5

8

9

10

MATERIALS LIST			
Item	Material	Size (in mm)	No.
Base	9 mm Craftwood*	350 x 500	1
Side	9 mm Craftwood	40 x 484	2
End	9 mm Craftwood	90 x 316	2

Other. 25 mm particle board screws; PVA glue; wood filler; particle board sealer; paint.
* Plywood of a similar thickness may be used as an alternative.

LETTERBOX

Cut out all the components, using materials list. Use a fine drill and fretsaw to cut the 150 x 100 mm door in the back. Cut the letter slot in the front — as the photograph indicates — with a 20 mm drill bit and fretsaw. Cut the roof curves in the front and back gables using the drawings as a guide. Saw 18 mm rebates 118 mm down the back and front edges of the sides to allow the front and back of the box to slot into them. Assemble the letterbox using nails and wood glue; taper the side edges of the internal base to accommodate the slope of the sides and fit to the box. Similarly, taper the bottom and screw to the top of the post.

Use a hard edge and metal scoring tool to incise deep lines around the metal sheet 10 mm in from the edges. Use the hard edge and a mallet to fold all edges along the scored lines. Use a metal pipe or timber dowel to roll the central curve in the roof and fix the sheet in place with 20 mm clouts. Hinge door and fix catch in place. Mark out and saw the two curved brackets and screw them to the post and letterbox for extra stability. Bury the creosoted post one-third into the ground.

PATRIOTIC HOUSE NUMBER

Give your home a patriotic appeal with a fair dinkum number plate. Use an offcut of 25 mm-thick timber (the number plate in the picture used a piece about 450 x 320 mm. Trace or draw the outline of Australia on the timber and cut out with a fretsaw. Finish with paint and brass numbers, or leave the timber plain and paint on the numbers. Fix to the wall with countersunk screws.

MATERIALS LIST

Item	Materials	Length or size (in mm)	No.
Front and back	200 x 18 mm Western Red Cedar	230 x 185	1 each
Sides	200 x 18 mm Western Red Cedar	300 x 175	2
Internal base	200 x 18 mm Western Red Cedar	265 x 165	1
Bottom	200 x 18 mm Western Red Cedar	300 x 185	1
Brackets	200 x 18 mm Western Red Cedar	200 x 120	2
Post	42 x 42 mm Cedar	1500 mm or to suit	1

Other. 350 x 320 galvanised tin plate; two 25 mm fixed pin hinges; one small hasp and staple catch; 35 mm jolt head nails; 50 mm countersunk screws; 20 mm clouts; wood glue.

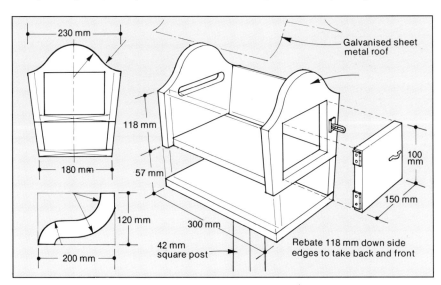

SHOE-SHINE CADDY

Materials. 1.5 m of 200 x 19 (or 25) mm pine; 200 mm of 25 x 25 mm pine for handle, all DAR; 30 mm panel pins; white glue; two decorative hinges and screws.
Method. Cut timber as in the diagram. Scribe an arc on the ends of the two legs and cut with a jigsaw. Where the lid is hinged, slope the edges as in the diagram. Assemble with panel pins and glue. Temporarily position the lid and mark holes for screws in the lid and fixed top. Drill holes for screws, and screw the hinges in place. Glue and pin the heel rest in place.

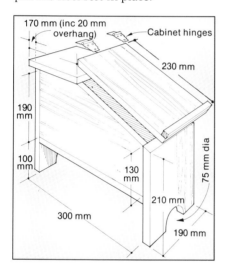

TURRET PLANTER

Conceal a flower pot in this unusual turret planter. Cut four 300 mm-square panels from 13 mm particle board. Draw 75 mm-diameter circles on two top corners of one panel. On each side draw a line, 12 mm in from edge, from bottom of panel to bottom of circle; draw a line between the circles 235 mm from bottom of panel. Repeat for remaining three panels. To half-lap panels together, cut a 13 mm slot half the length of each panel on each side, so that two have cuts from the top and two from the bottom. Cut along side lines, around circles and across line between circles. Sand edges. Fit panels together so they're flush top and bottom. Paint.

MOULDINGS

FINISHES WITH A TOUCH OF CLASS

The modern home, for all its efficiency and time- and energy-saving appliances, often lacks the refinement of details which are the signals of quality in old houses. The plain sweeps of plasterboard and quarter curve cornices which shape the uninspiring interiors of most mass-produced housing are a fitting background for embellishment. It is quite possible to add stylish finish to decor with minimum cost and effort using readily available timber mouldings. These mouldings come in many styles, and ranges vary from one timber yard to the next. Specialist suppliers in the larger cities have built up stocks of architectural trims and details which exactly match the originals in older houses. By putting together different profiles, interesting effects can be created.

As well as adding beauty to walls, mouldings can be applied around windows and used to decorate furniture and built-ins to great effect. Those with a penchant for the quieter life will probably elect to colour added mouldings to match the background, be it wall or whatever. However, there is an opportunity here for making an interesting statement in colour. Strong shades such as a clear red or black will define and delineate the moulding and make it appear to stand away from its surround. A more subtle approach would be to colour the trim with related shades or strike up a variation on a pastel theme.

An elaborately framed window using mouldings to great effect

AROUND WALLS

Use mouldings to break up expanses of wall and to correct difficult proportions in a room.

Accent different sections of a wall by adding beaded panels about 100 mm inside the perimeter.

Include a moulded dado at one-third wall height and add similar moulded surrounds to built-ins. Finish with white paint.

Divide a room into horizontal bands by using timber mouldings at the skirting, the dado, the picture rail and the cornice. This will present the opportunity to make colour changes, grading from slightly darker at the bottom to mid-tone around the central section and white or a pale shade at the top and for the ceiling. If ceilings are low, drop the height of the dado, eliminate the picture rail and make the skirting no more than 75 mm deep.

ON CUPBOARDS

Improve old-fashioned, cheap or just plain boring cupboards (and other furniture) by adding moulded strips at the critical points.

Make a series of shapes by framing each drawer or cupboard door with simple 35 mm wide maple cover stripping.

Crown the top of the freestanding cupboard by adding a square section of timber and mouldings beneath and along the front of it.

Revamp the plainest of cupboards by giving it the beaded treatment. Glue off-the-shelf scrolled moulding across the top, then around the three remaining sides add a similarly fine but straight beading, stopping a little short of the top piece at both ends. Nail a 30 mm-deep moulded edge around the edge of the bench, checking the depth against the door swing.

AROUND AN OPENING

Frame windows and doors with simple or elaborate timber trims for an elegant finish.

Separate windows with pilasters made of planks with moulded tops and bases and beaded front panels.

Add a clever variation to door and window surrounds with square blocks replacing mitred corners.

Finish windows with peaked pelmets, trimmed across the top.

Smarten up an architrave simply by adding a decorative moulding to the outside of the existing timber framework. Choose a fairly florid style, especially if the window and door surrounds are very plain. Cover windows with simple blinds rather than elaborate and expensive curtains; these will let the fancy mouldings do the talking.

ON A MANTELPIECE OR SHELF

Add traditional flair to shelving by including the detailing that only moulding can give.

Make the simple fire surround with three levels of flat timber and scotia moulding tacked into the resulting steps. Trim the edge of the mantelpiece and beneath it with a combination of mouldings.

Start with 250 mm-wide planks for the mantel shelf and back. Add jigsawed supports between and trim with appropriate mouldings.

AS FRAMES

You can build frames using any available moulding. Although the mitre joint needs practice before perfection is reached, wood filler and paint will hide the amateur's mistakes.

To make a frame of a complicated shape, mark the outline on a piece of board and lay the moulding in place to mark the angles of the cuts.

Construct more complicated frames by making a stepped formwork of flat sections of timber first. It is best to try out the combination in the timber yard or use small offcuts. On the flat steps, build up an individually 'antique' frame using shaped mouldings, scotia or quad in the corners of the flat-backed trims.

ARCHITECTURAL MIRROR

This framed mirror was inspired by the doorway joinery of early houses and reflects the view of the outdoors through the room's only exit to the garden. It gives a much needed impression of light and space to this small and rather dark living area. Proportions and detailing are in the style of Georgian architraves but could just as easily match or closely imitate doorway openings in houses from other eras.

To make the frame use 150 x 19 mm pine for the two verticals and 200 x 19 mm for the top horizontal, lap joining them at the top two corners to make an inverted U. Use 30 mm-long countersunk screws to secure the joints. The frame rests on an L-shaped aluminium extrusion which supports the bottom edge of the mirror.

Drill and screw fix the frame to the wall. Include the strip of aluminium at the bottom.

Stand the mirror in place using strong cloth-based adhesive tape to secure it temporarily. Using the photograph as a guide, trim the basic structure of the frame with architectural mouldings ensuring that the mouldings on the verticals are a little wider than the frame. Allow the inner edges of the fluted verticals to overlap the mirror in order to hold the mirror in place. Wedge pieces of matchstick in the gaps between mirror and mouldings to hold the mirror firmly.

Include blocks the height of skirtings. Those in the photograph are simply rectangles the width of the mouldings decorated with a groove cut by a router.

See drawing for the combination of beading and scotia to make up the top. Mitre corners of these

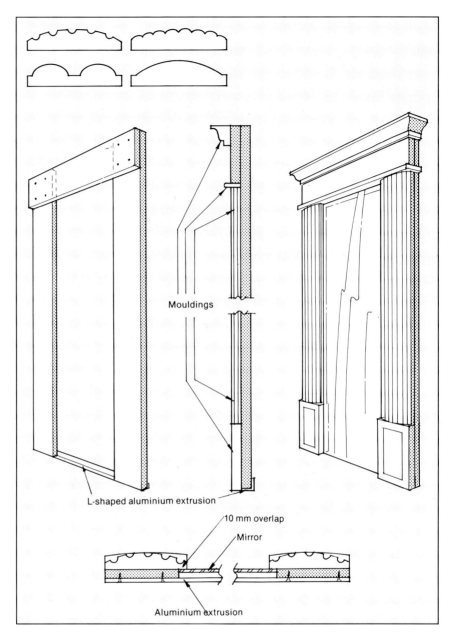

Mouldings

L-shaped aluminium extrusion

10 mm overlap

Mirror

Aluminium extrusion

mouldings for the depth of the frame.

Fix all decorative timber to the frame with countersunk screws. Leave mirror frame in raw state as in the photograph or finish as desired with paint, clear polyurethane or a limed wash. A limed wash is a thin coat of either plastic or oil-based paint, rubbed back with a clean cloth while still wet to leave a suggestion of colour (usually a pale shade) without totally obscuring the grain of the timber.

THE WORKSHOP

ORGANISING THE PERFECT WORKPLACE

Smooth the path to successful, enjoyable and rewarding weekend projects by plotting and planning a well equipped workshop. Even if the space for such a room is not much bigger than a toolbox, organisation is the keyword. Establish a proper place for every piece of equipment and remember that little items are more likely to go astray than the big ones. Always keep the chuck key for changing the drill bit tied on to the cord or body of your power drill or it will disappear. Measuring tapes and needle-nosed pliers also have well-earned reputations for being elusive. In fact any tool which is used regularly by different members of the family is likely to be misplaced. Have back-up supplies of popular tools and try to buy them in bright, even fluorescent, colours. With the workbench, the pivotal point of the workshop, never skimp on size and weight. It needs to be solid and very stable.

Make way for a workshop or utility area in the house where tools and materials can be stored. Floorplans of average homes rarely allow for such a space so it is usually up to the resident home-maintenance and carpentry expert to find one. A workshop could be built under a pitched roof, attic style, or placed between the piers beneath the house. Or perhaps there is a basement, laundry or even a space under the stairs which could be replanned as a work area.

Ideally, a workshop should be dry, cool and reasonably soundproof, especially if it is located close to the living quarters of the house or the neighbouring property. It should also have excellent natural and artificial light, good cross ventilation (fumes of paints, finishes and various preparations can be not only unpleasant, but dangerous as well), power points (preferably at bench height), a sturdy workbench at hip height for maximum efficiency, a practical floor finish which won't be spoiled by inevitable spills, and suitable storage for all hardware paraphernalia. If the floor is concrete, have a rubber mat over an offcut of underfelt in front of the workbench for comfort underfoot. Although the workshop is not meant to be luxuriously appointed or a gathering place for wits and scholars, a simple chair or stool (or two) is a good idea for solo tea breaks or when a visitor drops in.

A well equipped and arranged workshop

COMMONSENSE AND SAFETY IN THE WORKSHOP

• Develop the habit of wearing safety glasses in the workshop.

• Clean up at the end of each workshop session.

• Wear a face mask when sweeping and vacuuming to get rid of sawdust and dirt.

• Read labels on preparations carefully. Some tasks involving potentially dangerous substances are best performed outside.

• Keep instruction books for equipment close to hand on a shelf

or in a drawer.
• Have power tools serviced.
• Sharpen cutting edges of hand tools; blunt blades are inefficient and dangerous.
• Keep sharp tools and poisonous preparations out of reach of children.
• When using tools, keep calm. Haste and bad temper are disastrous in the workshop.
• Unplug tools before leaving the workshop. Fit the door to the room with a lock.
• Clear the floor of obstacles. Carelessly placed extension cords can be tripwires in the workshop.
• Have a fire extinguisher close by.

Planning a program of weekend projects also means finding plenty of space away from general family activity. A corner of the garage or shed where surfaces can cope with tough treatment is ideal. Make use of the area under the work surface by fitting it with shelves for planks of timber and sheets of leftover plastic laminate and particle board. A vice is an essential piece of workshop equipment and needs to be securely attached to a flush-finished (no overhang) benchfront. Pegboards can cope with tools and screws and nails are conveniently kept in tiny, see-through drawers.

When the only space to spare is in the spare room, a wall can be converted to a workshop. The prefabricated kit bench is slender so it won't get the guest. Pegboard with shelf above is generous in size and capacity.

Devotees of chisel, lathe and drill need space and as a result, the family car can be out in the cold. Batten down the roller shutter door and use it as a pegboard.

As a tool collection grows, the collectors devise new and ingenious methods of storage. This drilled and slotted board is just the job for screwdrivers, chisels and rasps.

WORKBENCH

No workbench? Use this dimensional drawing as a guide to make one. Adjust the height to suit your own stature and make the top flush with the front if a vice is to be installed.

SAWHORSES

Essential to the serious handyman, this pair of sturdy sawhorses is made from inexpensive pine. They'll make the job of cutting timber much easier because their height allows the body to bend over the work so maximum strength can be put into the job.

To saw the angles accurately you will need a power saw set into its bench. If you have this facility, cut all the angles at 15° outside the right angle. If you are not able to do this, cut the housing recesses in the top at 90° and allow the angled braces to set the legs at the correct slope.

Cut the housings with a saw, hammer and chisel into the top piece in the positions indicated on the diagram. Cut the legs about 25 mm longer than necessary and set them in the housings, protruding above the top surface.

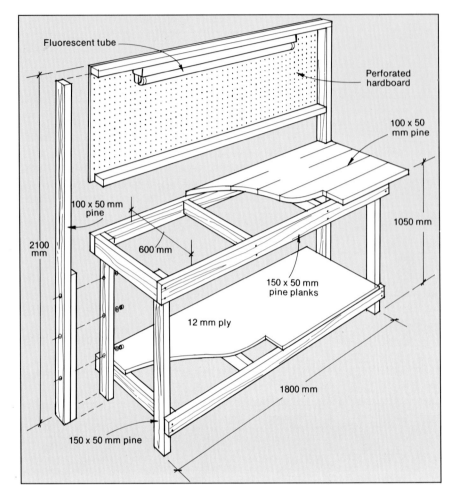

Saw them off level with the top last of all. Screw through the braces into the edges of the legs and through the legs into the housing, using 55 mm screws in the positions indicated in the diagram.

The splayed legs will stop the sawhorses from toppling over no matter how much weight may be applied to them.

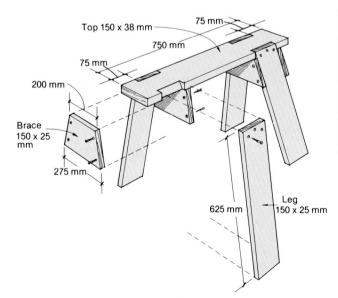

Drill. Most jobs call for holes to be drilled. Everything, from inserting screws to starting saw cuts that do not extend to the edge of the timber, is made much easier with a power drill and a good selection of drill bits. One recommended optional extra is a variable speed control, which enables drilling into materials of different densities.

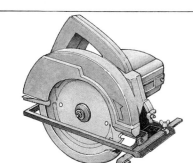

Circular Saw. Though most saw cuts can be made with a hand saw, a power saw will save a lot of time and energy, especially when using hardwoods. A saw with a 185 mm diameter blade (approximately) will be sufficient for the amateur. Though power saws are noisy and sometimes forbidding, their blade guards ensure that the cutting edge is covered when not in use.

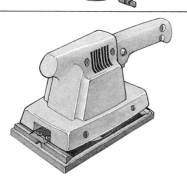

Orbital Sander. This is a wonderful companion when it comes to finishing any work. Any job is only as good as the finished surface and using a sander is the quickest way to achieve a smooth appearance. It allows the filling and smoothing off of any blemishes in timber and plaster surfaces alike and conceals inaccuracies in building projects.

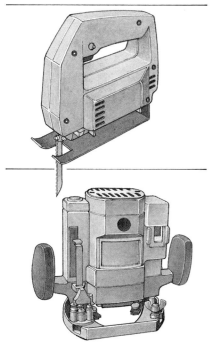

Jigsaw. This relatively modern invention opens up a whole new world to the home handyman. It allows the making of curved cuts in just about any material. Also, because its blade is narrow and short, saw cuts can be made in places that would otherwise be too confined. Being able to saw circles and irregular curves allows a greater range of design options.

Router. The strongest joints incorporate rebates (recesses in one piece of timber into which the abutting component fits). The router provides the only quick and accurate method of cutting a rebate. It has a guide at the side which you set on the edge of the timber to keep the cutting tip evenly positioned.

POWER TOOLS

Although all building tasks can be performed with hand tools, using electrical energy rather than the human variety will allow you to get the job done more quickly and, in most cases, more accurately.

These days, power tools are available in different capacities. Most manufacturers produce a light-capacity range which is adequate for weekend projects. The tools are shown in order of priority.

A drill is essential. It is almost impossible to undertake any building project without drilling holes.

A circular saw is a must for work with any wood except small-dimensioned timber.

An orbital sander is invaluable for giving work a professional finish. Most drills have a disc attachment to take circular sheets of sandpaper and act as a power sander, but this tends to leave curved marks in softer surfaces.

The jigsaw allows you to perform a wider range of building activities, and in some cases it can do the work of the circular or disc saw.

The router, used to cut rebates in timber for stronger joints, should be your last purchase. Make do with simple timber joints until you become more experienced.

HAND TOOLS – A BASIC SET

With the right tools, any job can be tackled. Basic hand tools haven't changed all that much since grandpa's day although plastic handles, retractable tape measures and planes show the signs of technological advance. Old tools discovered in the course of cleaning out the workshop should be treasured. They are highly prized by collectors and sometimes of better quality than today's equivalents.

1. Coping saw. Ideal for cutting curves and intricate joints. Blades are replaceable.
2. Panel saw. For cutting larger pieces of timber to size. Use a small file to sharpen individual teeth.
3. Tenon saw. For cutting joints, such as mitres.
4. Oilstone. For sharpening chisels and blade knives.
5. Adjustable spanners. These ensure that you will always have a tight fit on a nut. Use bolts and nuts for connecting large timber pieces.
6. Hand drill. Handy for small jobs such as making screw holes.
7. G-clamps. For anchoring your timber to the workbench while you saw it. You can also clamp timber together during construction.
8. Mitre box. Sets the saw blade at the exact 45° or 90° angle.
9. Plane. To finish your timber to any dimension. You can adjust the blade to alter the depth of the cut.
10. Twist bits. Allow you to drill up to 15 mm with your hand drill. Flat bits will drill larger holes.
11. Spirit level. For checking that all surfaces are exactly horizontal or vertical.

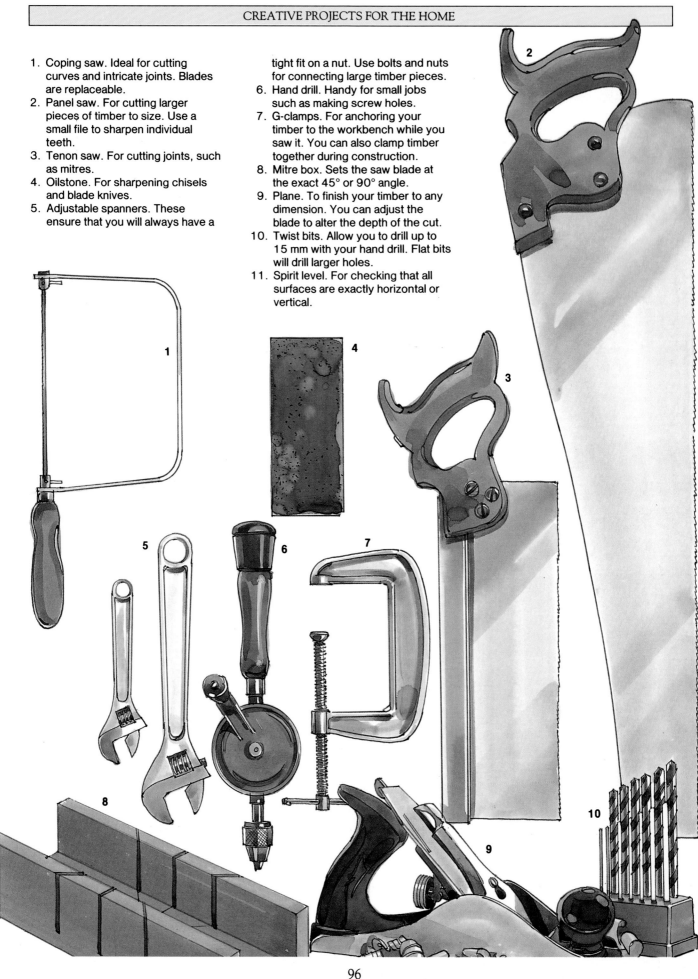

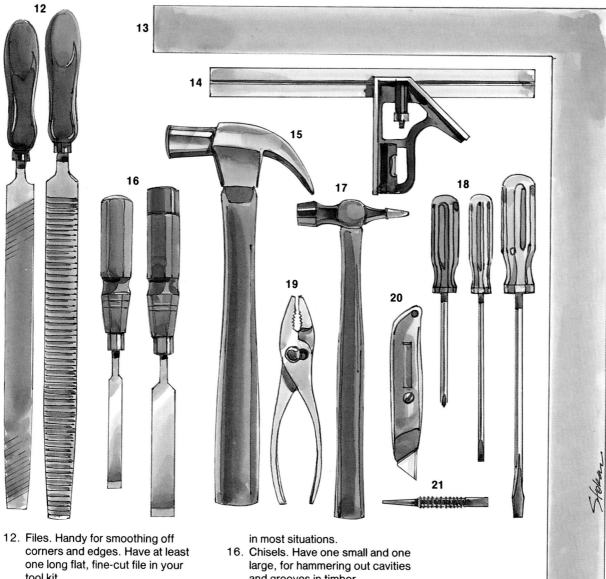

12. Files. Handy for smoothing off corners and edges. Have at least one long flat, fine-cut file in your tool kit.

13. Framing square. For marking out shapes on large sheets and checking large-scale right angles.

14. Combination square. Makes quick work of marking out 90° and 45° angles and checking for accuracy with the in-built spirit level at the same time.

15. Curved claw hammer. For hammering in and levering out nails in most situations.

16. Chisels. Have one small and one large, for hammering out cavities and grooves in timber.

17. Tack hammer. For small nails and pins in tight situations.

18. Screwdrivers. Buy these as you need them, making sure that the tool fits the screw head exactly.

19. Pliers. For tightening bolts, cutting wires and gripping and removing nails.

20. Trimming knife. Useful for cutting all materials as well as adjusting cuts in your timber components.

21. Nail punch. You may need to buy more than one of these to allow you to recess different size nail heads into your timber.

22. Tape measure. Simply indispensable.

JOINT TECHNIQUES

Joining two pieces of timber together is the basis of most of the projects illustrated in this book. Here are some of the simplest joints, clearly drawn and explained. Try them out with scrap timber, using off-cuts of the same thickness for each one. All joints should be glued and nailed or screwed.

1. Butt. This is the most basic of timber joints and the most frequently used. Execute it by simply butting the two timber surfaces together and fixing one component onto the end of the other. Glue and screws or nails give the joint its only strength.

2. Rebated. You will achieve greater strength if you cut a rebate into one piece of timber and position the adjoining piece in it. Cut vertically across the timber grain with a coping or tenon saw (these are more rigid saws that give you greater control) to the depth of the rebate, and use a hammer and chisel to remove the waste timber.

3. Half-Lap. Use your saw, hammer and chisel for this method also. By cutting recesses into both components to a depth of half the thickness of the timber, you will make a very strong joint. This type is most often used for timber joined over its horizontal dimension.

4. Lap. Where the two timbers do not have to finish flush with one another, this basic lap-joint will suffice. It is vital that you locate screws or nails diagonally across the joint as this gives the joint its strength.

5. Brackets. Concealed steel brackets of different sizes and shapes may be used to reinforce any timber joint. You should also nail or screw through the joint as for any butt joint.

6. Mitre. When you require a perfect finish and the joint is to be

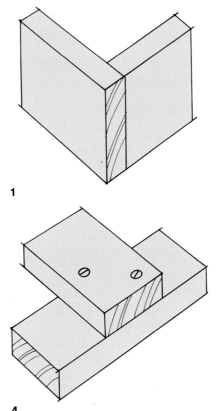

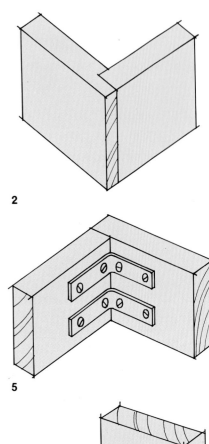

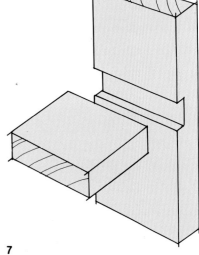

left exposed, you should use a mitre-joint. You will need a mitre box and tenon saw to ensure the two cuts are at exactly 45 degrees. A mitre cramp is useful to hold the two components in place while you glue and nail them together. Insert the nails at alternating angles to stop the joint pulling apart.

7. Housed. When making a T-joint (stronger than the butt), saw and chisel a groove or housing into one component and allow the adjoining timber to sit into it. Start the groove by sawing downwards across the grain, making two parallel cuts through half the thickness of the timber. Chisel out the recess between them.

8. Butt with Block. If your basic butt-joint is not strong enough for the job, reinforce it with a cleat on the inside of the corner. This makes a very practical joint which you should use whenever appearance is not the main consideration. Screw

through both the components into the corner block.

9. Mortice and Tenon. This is the strongest way to make a T-joint. Saw the tenon or tongue to fit into the mortice or slot of the other component. Both mortice and tenon should be one-third the thickness of the timber. You will have to use a sharp chisel to cut the mortice accurately.

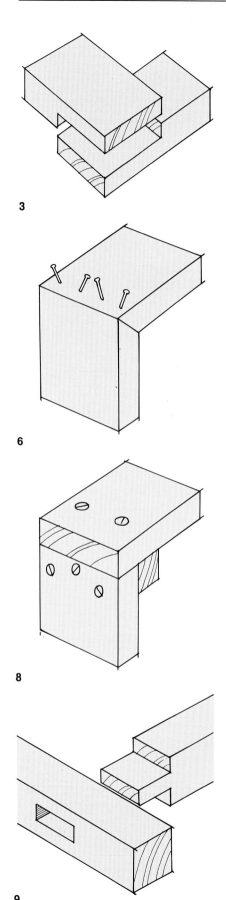

3

6

8

9

THE FINISHING TOUCH

A professional standard of finish depends on preparing the surface properly before varnishing, waxing or painting.

FILLING

Fillers vary from acrylic compounds (purely cosmetic cover-up fillers) to epoxy resins which bond with timber, and take screws and nails.

Punch nails and countersink screws with a countersunk drill bit; then use filler to disguise the heads. Smooth furry end grain by filling and sanding. Also conceal knots, splits and grain blemishes with filler. Despite claims to the contrary, all fillers shrink to some extent when drying. For deep cavities, build up layers, allowing each one to dry before proceeding. Sand top flush with timber surface.

Colouring may be difficult as fillers often take in more stain than timber. Although there are fillers already tinted to match most common timber types, naturally there are variations. Test coloured filler on the underside of a project before proceeding.

PLUGGING

A plug gives an ultra-flush finish over a countersunk screw. After drilling the hole for the screw, use an ordinary drill bit the width of the screw head and drill to a depth of 10mm below the surface. (A countersunk drill bit cannot make a hole as deep as this.) Cut a same width dowel plug a little shorter than the depth of the hole, tap it in place and sand flush.

A system comprising a plastic cap with a conical component through which the screw shaft is inserted is another method of concealing screw and bolt heads.

EDGING

Timber edging strips conceal the end grains of timber, timber-veneered particle board and plain particle board sawn edges. Have them the same width as the sheet material, or deeper for a more substantial look. Glue and tack the strips in place and fill and sand the junction. Paint them to match or clear finish them as a feature detail. Pine edging strips combine well with white or coloured plastic-laminated particle board.

Heat-bonded strips in a basic range of timber types and colours for timber-veneered and plastic-laminated particle board give professional quality edges. A household iron provides the necessary heat source.

SANDING

Wrap sandpaper around a cork or timber block and always sand with the grain. To smooth down rough timber and end grain, start with a medium-grade sandpaper and work through a couple of lighter grades. Use a light-grade paper between coats of paint and varnish.

An orbital sander makes it easier to achieve a good finish. Keep sander running along the grain or squiggle marks will occur.

STAINING

Work quickly and evenly, covering the entire surface with stain before it dries. Use a soft cloth or brush for application and work in the direction of the grain. Wipe off excess with a clean dry cloth and when dry, wipe again before applying a clear coating. Practise on a scrap of the same timber first.

Choose a stain that is compatible with the finish you have in mind; check with the supplier before purchasing. Most stains produce denser colours than expected.

TIMBER AND BOARDS

Definitions of timber can leave the novice blinking in confusion. Hardwood and softwood seem to be straightforward enough as descriptive terms. However, the botanist and the carpenter or cabinetmaker have different opinions. Tradespeople use these terms literally to describe timber that is either hard or soft to work. In the realms of science, hardwood can include species as different as balsa and ironbark, and also includes Pacific Maple — an old 'softie' from way back. In fact botanists rate the term 'hardwood' as an inaccurate botanical description.

It is possible to buy timber from mills in widths and thicknesses limited only by the size of the tree, but standard sizes available in timber yards and hardware shops are more economical and easier to obtain. In the case of sheet materials, ask the local supplier about sheet sizes available to minimise waste and maximise the purchase.

Although timber is cut and sheet materials produced in an astounding variety of thicknesses, widths and lengths, a retail outlet will only keep those sizes for which there is the most demand. Sometimes it is worth going to a larger timber yard or building supplier to find sizes of materials suited to specific needs. Timber is sold by the linear metre so estimate the length of each type needed before ordering.

All timber except pine is sold in its nominal or undressed dimensions. When it is dressed, that is, planed smooth, its dimensions are considerably reduced. For instance, a piece of timber measuring 100 x 38 mm will be 90 x

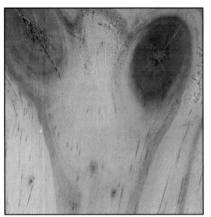

1   Radiata Pine

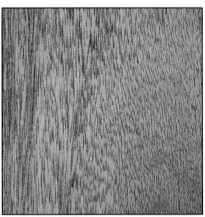

2   Pacific Maple

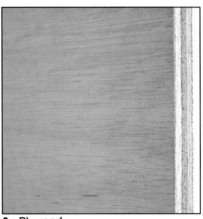

6   Plywood

7   Hardboard

30 mm when dressed — referred to as dressed-all-round or DAR or sometimes S4S.

The amount by which the timber is reduced when it is planed smooth varies with different timber types and different milling equipment. Pine is sold in its dressed sizes

Radiata Pine. Radiata Pine from New Zealand and Slash Pine from Queensland are the least expensive natural timbers on the market. The nature of the grain makes it flex as well as splinter when sawn. The grain has very high contrast and in some situations needs to be painted. It is ideal for furnishings and shelving. Unless it is preservative-treated, Radiata Pine is not suitable for outside use.
Thickness: 19–90 mm
Widths: 19–290 mm

Pacific Maple. Pacific Maple is soft to work and commonly used. The closeness of its grain makes it easy to work and sand to a smooth finish. It is strictly an interior timber and is

particularly suitable for furniture and joinery.
Thickness: 13–50 mm
Widths: 25–300 mm

Oregon. Oregon is a high-quality timber which, when properly treated, can be used for exterior applications such as pergolas and other garden structures. It has traditionally been used for house framework but cheaper materials have now made their way into this area.
Thickness: 25–100 mm
Widths: 50–300 mm

Western Red Cedar. Western Red Cedar is the most expensive timber available. It is durable in all exterior conditions. Its natural colour makes it even more appealing and it will weather to a pale grey when left untreated. Its softness can be a disadvantage.
Thickness: 19–100 mm
Widths: 25–300 mm

Hardwood. High density hardwoods are often rated *highly* durable in-ground (e.g. tallowwood, ironbark, white mahogany) but others such as Tasmanian Oak (really 'ash' type

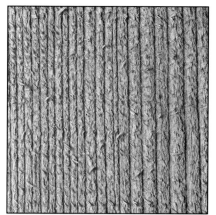

3 Oregon

4 Western Red Cedar

5 Hardwood

8 Dowelling

9 Particle Board

10 Plastic-laminated particle board

eucalypts) and Pacific Maple are ranked as *non*-durable.
Thickness: 25–150 mm
Widths: 25–250 mm

Plywood. Plywood, which is bonded layers of timber, varies in size, quality and thickness. Because it is composed of layers, plywood comes in sizes wider than 300 mm. The layers give the sheets strength.
Plywood that is 4, 6 and 9 mm thick comes in sheet sizes 1800, 2100 and 2400 mm long; these lengths are available in 900 and 1200 mm widths.
7, 12 and 17 mm thicknesses:
2400 x 1200 mm
19 mm-thick form ply (exterior grade):
2500 x 1200 mm

Hardboard. This dark composite board is a relatively dense material. It has no structural capacity and should be used only where it is supported by a frame. Hardboard forms an excellent underlay for floor coverings. One side is smooth, the other rough. Pictured is the rough back surface.
5.5 mm thicknesses: 1800 x 1200 mm, 2400 x 900 mm, 2400 x 1200 mm

Dowelling. This material is useful in forming uprights and joining components in building projects.
Thicknesses of 6, 8, 10, 12.5, 16, 19, 25, 35 and 44 mm: all available in 1.8 m lengths. The 19 to 44 mm thicknesses are available in 2.4 m lengths.

Particle Board. Particle board is only suitable for interior use. It is composed of timber chips or particles formed with glues and pressure into a sheet. Only the surfaces of the sheets are smooth and you will usually have to glue and nail timber edging onto the rough sheet edges. Particle board requires special screws with straight-threaded shanks for better gripping power.
Thickness: 13 mm
Sheets: 900 x 450 mm —
               2700 x 1500 mm
Thickness: 19 mm
Sheets: 900 x 450 mm —
               3600 x 1800 mm

Plastic-laminated particle board is ideal for situations where a wipedown surface is an advantage. Its white sheen gives any project executed in it a

contemporary appearance. The rough-sawn edges can be covered with iron-on plastic edging strips.
Thickness: 16 mm
Sheets: 1800 x 600 mm and
               2400 x 1200 mm
Thickness: 4mm
Sheets: 1200 x 900 mm and
               2400 x 1200 mm
Thickness: 6 mm
Sheets: 2400 x 1200 mm

Medium-density fibre board is a new material with extra density which allows you to screw into its end grain. Sawn edges require no finish other than sanding and painting.
Thicknesses: 13 and 18 mm
Sheets: 2400 x 900 mm,
               2400 x 1200 mm
               1800 x 900 mm,
               1800 x 1200 mm

INDEX

Published by **Murdoch Books**, a division of Murdoch Magazines Pty Ltd
213 Miller Street, North Sydney NSW 2060

Manuscript Development: Diane Wallis
Design: Warren Penney
Illustrations and Diagrams: David Stokan
Finished Art: Ivy Hansen
Cover Photograph: Rodney Weidland

Publisher: Anne Wilson
Production Manager: Penny Martin
Managing Editor: Maureen Colman
Marketing Manager: Mark Smith

National Library of Australia
Cataloguing-in-Publication Data
Creative Projects for the Home
ISBN 0 86411 143 6
Includes index.
1. Dwellings — maintenance and repair. 2. Landscape
gardening. 3. Garden structures. 4. Interior decoration
(Series: Australian Better Homes and Gardens Homemaker Library).
643.7

First published 1990
Printed by Griffin Press Ltd, Netley, SA
Typeset by Savage Type Pty Ltd, Brisbane, Qld.
© Murdoch Books 1990

Australian distribution to supermarkets and newsagents by
Gordon & Gotch Ltd, 68 Kingsgrove Road, Belmore NSW 2192

* Recommended and maximum price only